GUIDE TO
MARXIST PHILOSOPHY

An Introductory Bibliography

GUIDE TO

MARXIST PHILOSOPHY

An Introductory Bibliography

Edited by

Joseph M. Bochenski

and

Frederick J. Adelmann   Daniel J. McCarthy
Thomas J. Blakeley   Patrick McNally
Gervase J. Cain   James J. O'Rourke
Augustine Lin   Charles M. Savage
James May

THE SWALLOW PRESS INC.

CHICAGO

First edition
    First printing

Published by
The Swallow Press Incorporated
1139 South Wabash Avenue
Chicago, Illinois 60605

This book is printed on 100% recycled paper

ISBN (clothbound edition) 0-8040-0560-5
ISBN (paperbound edition) 0-8040-0561-3
LIBRARY OF CONGRESS CATALOG CARD NUMBER 76-188168

CONTENTS

PREFACE

Marxism is justifiably a subject of widespread interest, for it constitutes the theoretical basis of several powerful political organizations. It is also not devoid of purely philosophical interest. The result is that many students want to learn about it, and many schools have special courses on Marxism.

Unfortunately, the study of Marxism and especially of the philosophical aspect of Marxism has been the subject of much misleading literature, written either by people who do not know the subject, or by propagandists, who do not aim at presenting it as it is, but at gaining sympathizers. On the other hand, while other aspects of Marxism (political economy, social science, etc.) are perhaps in a better position, Marxist philosophy has been studied very little; consequently, there are few teachers really competent in it. This is not always their fault. The demand for courses on Marxism is so great that often otherwise respectable scholars have been induced to teach a subject they do not know very well. Also, a knowledge of Marxism involves a considerable effort: the mastery of several foreign languages, of complex historical and doctrinal backgrounds, etc. The result is that in too many cases the teaching of Marxism is inadequate, to put it mildly. To quote just one instance: I have seen recently a rather ample bibliography on Marxism given to students at a respectable American university. It contained some 200 titles, but (a) not a single writing of Lenin, (b) practically no mention of any serious Western work on Marxist philosophy, (c) a great number of books by authors only as well informed as the unfortunate teacher who compiled that bibliography. Obviously, students led in such a way can only be misled; they will never understand what Marxism is.

The present book was written in order to supply such students with a very simple and practical guide to the field. The idea was conceived by the undersigned during his stay in Dover, Massachusetts, in the fall of 1970. Having met a number of Sovietologists and Marxologists, chiefly through Professor Thomas Blakeley, Director of the Russian Philosophical Studies Program at Boston College, he submitted to them the project of writing in common such a guide. The idea was amply discussed, accepted, and elaborated, both in the meetings of the group and in the criticism of the papers written by the individual members. The method followed was this: Each chapter was written by one or two members of the group, then submitted to all other members, who discussed it and offered suggestions. Thus the book is the result of a collective effort, and it was decided not to designate the authors of the first drafts.

The members of the team were: Professor Joseph M. Bochenski of the University of Fribourg (Switzerland), Professor Frederick J. Adelmann of Boston College, Professor Thomas J. Blakeley of Boston College, Professor Gervaise Cain of St. Francis College (Pennsylvania), Professor James O'Rourke of St. Anselm's College (New Hampshire), Mr. Daniel McCarthy of Boston State College, and the following graduate students of the Department of Philosophy at Boston College: Augustine Lin, James May, Patrick McNally, and Charles Savage.

As the book is a collective work, I do not think I have to thank the members of the team, in spite of the fact that, personally, I very much enjoyed working with them. But I only wish to express gratitude from all of us to Professor Blakeley, who was the chief organizer, and to Professor O'Rourke, who undertook the difficult task of editing and co-ordinating the manuscripts.

JOSEPH M. BOCHENSKI

1
INTRODUCTION

On Using This Book

This book is a guide to readings on Marxist philosophy, written for English-speaking students. It is a *guide to readings*, not an introduction to the doctrines themselves; only the necessary minimum has been said about the doctrines, in order to indicate the nature of the books recommended.

The subject matter is Marxist *philosophy*, not sociology, economics, or political science. It is true that it is sometimes difficult to separate the philosophy from the other doctrinal aspects of Marxism, but there definitely are purely philosophical aspects involved, and those have been the main interest here.

This guide is designed for those who read only *English*. Therefore, practically all books mentioned in it are written in English or exist in English translation. This is certainly a handicap, for much important literature exists only in other languages. However, the decision to refer only to English writings was taken in view of the fact that the prospective reader is assumed to have little knowledge of other languages.

Finally, it is a guide for those *beginning* their study of Marxist philosophy, those who have no serious acquaintance with Marxism.

Each chapter covers one type of Marxism. Each chapter contains three parts: a brief introduction, an indication of the writings appropriate for the beginner, and a more extensive list of books for further study. Although in some cases books may have more than one publisher (e.g., U.S.A. and England) or more than one edition, only one edition of any book is listed. Except where specifically noted, any available edition is satisfactory. Some books listed may be currently out of print (check the annual *Books in Print* volume, accessible for reference at libraries and bookstores) and therefore unavailable for purchase, but they can be obtained in any good library. An asterisk at the end of a title indicates a *paper*back edition.

The Varieties of Marxism

The term "Marxism" is used to refer to a vast class of doctrines, all of which claim to be legitimate interpretations and/or developments of the thought of Karl Marx. But while all of them contain at least some sociological, economic, or political doctrines drawn from Marxian writings, there is often little common among them as far as philosophy is concerned. In that respect, the various sorts of Marxism are often radically opposed one to the other. The term "Marxism" as referring to philosophy is, therefore, highly ambiguous and should never be used without qualification (e.g., Marxism-Leninism, Chinese Marxism).

The situation is rendered still more complex by the fact that the history of Marxism covers nearly one and a half centuries and that the doctrines were developed in at least three very different cultural frames of reference: German, Russian, and Chinese—to which one may add perhaps still others.

It is therefore necessary to make a clear distinction between several sorts of Marxism, or rather between the different meanings of the term "Marxism." At least the following should be distinguished:

1. The thought of *Karl Marx* himself is by itself a considerable field, worked out by specialists who are sometimes called Marxologists. The field offers a number of difficult problems, which cannot be properly understood and solved without a thorough knowledge both of Marx's sources and of his philosophical development. The thoughts of Marx may in some measure be illuminated by the work of Marx's followers, but the study must be concerned above all with the writings of Karl Marx himself. It is, in particular, quite wrong to try to understand Marx by reading Russian texts on dialectical materialism; or say, Marcuse's recent writings. One must read and analyze the works of Marx himself.

2. What can be called *German Classical Marxism* was founded by the

lifelong friend and collaborator of Marx, Friedrich Engels, and was further developed by a number of German Socialists, among whom Karl Kautsky is perhaps the most important. What came out of their work is a philosophy in many respects quite different from that of Marx himself. The main differences, as seen by recent Marxologists and emphasized by Neo-Marxians, can be summarized as follows: (a) While Marx explicitly rejected every intellectualistic, *speculative system* of philosophy and favored a *pragmatic* approach ("praxis"), Engels developed a speculative system. (b) While Marx favored an approach to philosophy which was called by Kolakowski *anthropocentric* (beginning with man, considering nature in reference to him), Engels' thought is clearly *cosmocentric*; it begins with the laws which are supposed to rule the world at large and only then proceeds to study man and society. (c) One doctrine which seems to have basic importance for Marx, namely the theory of *alienation*, is *practically ignored* by Engels.

However, because the philosophical writings of Marx were basically unknown in the 19th century (they are early works which were not published until the 20th century), the philosophy of Engels was falsely taken to be the same as that of his lifelong collaborator.

While classical Marxists developed the Engelsian philosophy, other Marxists tried to substitute for it another philosophical system, generally that of Immanuel Kant. One major representative of that trend is the so-called Reformism or Revisionism of Eduard Bernstein.

3. There is the thought of *Lenin*. A Russian, he was deeply influenced by the Russian revolutionary thinkers. Also, while embracing classical German Marxism, that is, while identifying Marx with Engels, he developed a number of personal ideas which gave to his philosophy a very particular shape. Lenin was, of course, not the only Russian Marxist of his time. He discussed, for example, the so-called Empiriomonism of Bogdanov and had some capable comrades in philosophy, such as Bukharin. However, it was Lenin who became the political leader of the Bolsheviks and his views prevailed in the Soviet Union.

4. Out of the thought of Lenin, the Russian Communists built up a vast body of doctrines, called by them *Marxism-Leninism*. There is a long and rather complex history of that philosophy. In spite of several changes

which occurred during a more than fifty year history, it retained, as a whole, its own characteristics which make it different from other types of Marxism.

5. In the countries which became Communist after the Second World War, at first there was no original philosophy; most works consisted of translations or repetitions of Russian writings. But since about 1953, an original form of Marxism has developed slowly in some of these countries. This fifth variety of Marxism is sometimes called (improperly) "Revisionism." A better term is *Neo-Marxism*. Its philosophical tenets are strongly opposed to those of Marxism-Leninism. Its partisans claim to go back to the authentic young Marx.

6. Another kind of Marxism seems to have developed in *China*, which has a completely different cultural background and whose main theoretician, Mao Tse-tung, proclaims his opposition to Soviet thought. This Marxism is, as yet, little developed, but as it seems to have some influence on Western thinking, it must be considered.

7. Finally, there is a class of Western European and American philosophers, who claim to develop one or another aspect of Marx's thought, while often rejecting other aspects. There is, philosophically, little common teaching in that class, which nevertheless is also called "Marxism." Sometimes the name *New Left* is given to it.

Schema

The development of the various Marxisms can be summarized by the following diagram, which represents the mutual dependence of the doctrines:

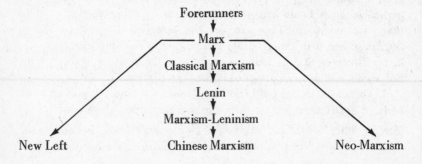

This scheme is incomplete, to the extent that it leaves out the respective background of each doctrine. There is, for example, a Russian background for both Lenin and Marxism-Leninism, a Chinese background for Maoism, and an East European background for Neo-Marxism. Nevertheless, the diagram does emphasize the relationships and the necessary presuppositions of the varieties of Marxism (e.g., Chinese Marxism presupposes Marxism-Leninism, while both presuppose Classical Marxism, etc.).

The following chronological summary indicates the life span of some of the most important Marxists. The asterisk indicates the year in which the thinker was thirty years old.

```
18                              19
10  20  30  40  50  60  70  80  90  00  10  20  30  40  50
───────────────────────────────────────────────────────────
Marx 1818-1883_____*
Engels 1820-1895 ___*
Labriola 1843-1904 _____*
Kautsky 1854-1938 _____*
Plekhanov 1856-1918 _____*
Lenin 1870-1924 _____*
Stalin 1879-1953 _____*
Kolakowski 1927- _____*
```

How to Study Marxism

Marxism is a set of doctrines. Whatever the peculiar characteristics of these doctrines might be, they are still theoretical systems and as such are objects of the study of the history of ideas (in so far as the philosophical aspect is concerned, of the history of philosophy). That is, *the general rules governing every study in the history of ideas have to be applied also to the study of Marxism.* There is no other way to know and to understand what Marxism really is. There are no short cuts; a systematic and controlled effort is needed.

The necessity of following such rules must be even more stressed here than in other fields, and this is for two reasons: first, because many emotions are connected with Marxism and tend to make one think about it in irrational ways, in wrong ways; second, because the field is unusally infected by bad literature, which purports to give information, while it does not. There are two kinds of such bad writings. One is produced by people who simply do not know and yet pretend to teach others; there is an amazing quantity of books on our subject written by such authors; this is probably due to the fact that so many people are vitally interested in the field. The other kind is worse still. These are writings published by propagandists, whose desire is not to instruct, but to gain partisans. In order to do so, they are very often ready to distort the Marxist doctrines, hoping that they might have more appeal to the ideals of the readers.

In view of this, it is highly important for the student to find the right way to begin his study. All too many students have been misled by bad literature. Often they wasted much time, and some were even permanently inhibited from acquiring any deep understanding of Marxism. Concretely, the student will do well to heed the following principles.

1. Do not read a book before being informed by a reliable authority that it is a good book. This rule is, of course, difficult to apply. But try.

2. Do not read authors who obviously are not genuine specialists in a field. For example, one may not know the language concerned; or one may be an excellent specialist on Karl Marx's early writings, but know practically nothing about Soviet Marxism.

3. First read an introduction to your subject. The present book is not such an introduction, but rather was meant to replace to some extent the reliable authority mentioned above. A good introduction read *before* reading the original texts will provide a survey of the field, will sketch the background, will outline the main teachings of the philosopher concerned and the history of the doctrines, and will point out which works are relevant to your study. If, for instance, one were to begin studying Marx's philosophy by reading his *Capital*, he would most certainly make a wrong start; there is very little philosophy in that work.

4. After an introduction, go to the original texts. No serious study in the history of philosophy, even on a beginning level, can be done without reading the original works of the philosopher(s) concerned. A beginner cannot read everything a philosopher wrote. How to select? Read at least one work in its totality, preferably a whole book or a long article. For

example, when studying Mao Tse-tung, read at least his papers *On Contradiction* and *On Practice*. For Engels, read the whole of *Ludwig Feuerbach*. Then read selections from your philosopher's other works. This will not give you a thorough knowledge of your author, but it will at least familiarize you with his thought; and it will help to avoid misunderstandings, which can result, especially from reading short pieces cut out of larger works by some editors of "Selections."

5. Then, and only then, read some good secondary sources, some discussions about your philosopher and his doctrines. Pay particular attention to the philosopher's background—his philosophical environment and his cultural milieu. The very meaning of terms used depends primarily on their cultural context. For instance, the American frame of reference and the Russian frame of reference may dictate completely different meanings for the same word. Know your philosopher's intellectual predecessors and contemporaries if at all possible. A serious study of, say, Adam Schaff, is severely weakened without at least some knowledge of the Polish Analytical School. Keep in mind that the greater the differences between your own culture and your own philosophical bent and that of the author studied, the more effort you must exert to gain insight into the history and culture in which that particular variety of Marxism developed; otherwise you will project into him your own background and understandings, and, of course, misinterpret him.

6. Do not trust men who are known to be primarily propagandists and not scholars. Do not trust a militant Communist, for Communists openly claim to be "party-men" and are known to distort the truth. The same warning also applies to militant anti-Communists, who are characterized more by their emotional attitude than by their knowledge. Of course, later on, the reading of such books (except those written by dilettantes) may be useful. But a beginning student should avoid them in order to hasten a true insight into the nature of Marxism.

The Beginner's Library

Only millionaires can afford to buy all the books they wish to read. Therefore, buy judiciously. There are easier ways to waste money than buying unnecessary books. In *buying* books, follow the same six principles outlined above about *reading* books. In other words, the first book to buy is a short, first-class introduction to the field in question. Then buy the works of your philosopher. Buy secondary literature only after you own original texts. Regardlesss of your field, you should own as many of the philosophical works as possible of Marx, Engels, and Lenin.

If you can avoid it, do not buy selections, but buy whole original works. There may be exceptions to this rule: for example, the philosophical writings of Karl Marx, which are few and may be available (complete) only in a set of selections. But the general rule is to avoid selections; they are good for dilettantes, not for serious students.

Here are some specific suggestions in three areas:

1. *Introductions.* There are very few if any books which can be recommended as introductions covering all varieties of Marxism as described. However, some introductions do cover much of the field: for instance, a good introduction to Marxism-Leninism, which also contains a historical survey of Marx himself, his sources, etc. At least two such books can be recommended:

Robert N. C. Hunt: *The Theory and Practice of Communism, An Introduction** (Baltimore, Penguin, 1963, 315 pp.). Hunt's work is probably the simplest, easiest and most readable—this without being superficial or, what is worse, wrong. This book should be the first reading of a student who is not yet trained in philosophical thinking, because Acton is considerably more technical.

H. B. Acton: *The Illusion of the Epoch: Marxism-Leninism as a Philosophical Creed* (London, Cohen & West, 1962, 278 pp.). Acton's book excels in clarity and systematic penetration of the doctrines he presents. It is considered one of the best of its kind.

2. *Reference Works.* Several well known encyclopedias contain some articles which can be fruitfully read as introductions to the field. The main ones are: the *Encyclopedia Britannica* and the *Encyclopedia of Philosophy*. Both contain far more than sketchy data. The writing was, in many cases, entrusted to first-class specialists, and the result is that some of the

articles are among the best in our field. These articles will also supply reliable data concerning biography and bibliography of the philosophers. The standard work covering at least a large part of our field is:

G.D.H. Cole: *A History of Socialist Thought* (London, Macmillan, 6 vols., 1955-1958). The material covered in the six volumes is broken down in the following way: vol. I, The Forerunners, 1789-1850; vol. II, Marxism and Anarchism, 1850-1890; vols. III-IV, The Second International, 1887-1914; vols. V-VI, Communism and Social Democracy 1914-1931. The work supplies mostly biographical and historical information; the author is not primarily interested in philosophy, yet his work may nevertheless be of value.

One special, very excellent reference work can render good service both to the beginning and to the advanced student.

John Lachs: *Marxist Philosophy, A Bibliographical Guide* (Chapel Hill, Univ. of North Carolina Press, 1967, 166 pp.). This work covers nearly the whole of our field. It quotes no fewer than 1,500 titles; and above all, it has in each of its thirty-six bibliographical chapters short but substantial introductions, in which the best books are mentioned and recommended, some with qualifications. It may be remarked that the author also lists bad books, so the fact that a title appears in his bibliography does not mean that the book is worth reading. This is one of the few books which every student could profit from owning.

3. *Journals.* Specialized journals are very important for advanced students; beginners will have less reason to use them. However, because some of them carry articles relevant for particular purposes and also for general orientation, a short list is given here. All journals mentioned are considered serious publications, which gives a certain authority to the articles published there.

Studies in Soviet Thought (Dordrecht, Holland, Reidel, 1960 ff.). This is probably the most important periodical publication in the field, and its relevance is not limited to the Soviet Union, as it also publishes contributions on Chinese and Neo-Marxist philosophy (e.g., the "Dialectical Materialism" of Mao Tse-tung was published in this journal). It publishes mostly reports and some texts, and a current bibliography of Soviet philosophy, the only of its kind. The first volume appeared as an issue of the series "Sovietica" (same publisher).

Survey, A Journal of Soviet and East-European Studies (London, Summit House, 1950 ff.). An important journal; it devotes more space to philosophy than most similar publications.

Praxis, A Philosophical Journal (Zagreb, Croatian Philosophical Society, 1965 ff.). This is the international edition (there is another in Serbo-Croatian); it is published partly in English. The content is purely philosophical and the standpoint Neo-Marxist.

Problems of Communism (Washington, D. C., United States Information Agency, 1952 ff.). This review contains mostly articles devoted to political and economic problems, with very few philosophical contributions. The level is generally high.

Slavic Review, American Quarterly of Soviet and East European Studies (Univ. of Illinois, American Association for the Advancement of Slavic Studies, 1941 ff.). A learned journal, with little material on philosophy.

Soviet Studies, A Quarterly Review of the Social and Economic Institutions of the USSR (Univ. of Oxford, Basil Blackwell, 1960 ff.). This is one of the best reviews in the field. It sometimes carries philosophical articles, but rarely. ·

Soviet Studies in Philosophy, A Journal of Translations (New York, International Arts and Sciences Press, 1962 ff.). This journal publishes exclusively translations of Soviet philosophical writings. The selection is not always that which might be desired, but it is one of the few publications which gives to those who cannot read Russian an access to Soviet writings.

Marxist books published overseas are not readily available at neighborhood bookstores in this country. Persons living in or near New York City, Chicago, San Francisco, or Washington, D. C. can find many Russian-published and Chinese-published books in English at the bookstores listed at the end of chapters 5 and 7. Other readers can order by mail from these same bookstores. A number of recommended books are published by Reidel in Holland. Books from Reidel and other European publishers (e.g., Nijhoff) can be obtained through any good bookstore, which will usually be happy to order overseas books.

2

PHILOSOPHICAL BACKGROUND

G. W. F. Hegel

The philosophy of G. W. F. Hegel (1770-1831) exerted a profound and lasting influence on the thought of Karl Marx and continued to shape the thought of his major disciples, including Engels, Lenin, and contemporary Soviet philosophers. The necessity for studying Hegel as a pre-condition for understanding the Marxist tradition was forcefully stated by Lenin, although in a somewhat exaggerated fashion: "It is impossible to understand Marx's *Capital* completely . . . without having thoroughly studied and understood the *whole* of Hegel's *Logic.*" It is not recommended that one begin his study of Marxism by reading Hegel's *Logic*, a difficult and abstract metaphysical treatise, but it is imperative to acquire at least a general understanding of Hegel's philosophical position. More precisely, it is the Hegelian method with which the student of Marxism should become familiar. In the somewhat oversimplified but yet helpful formulation which Marxists themselves give of their relation to Hegel, a division is made between, a) the doctrinal content of Hegel's philosophy, which is a monistic, objective idealism; and b) the dialectical method, most often presented as a form of process, or thought, moving from thesis to anti-thesis to synthesis. Marxists reject Hegel's objective idealism and enthusiastically embrace the dialectical method.

There is also a special sense in which Hegel is important in Marx's own philosophical development. Marx was thirteen years old when Hegel died, and the influence of this great thinker still largely dominated German university circles during Marx's early academic career. Marx was at one point a convinced Hegelian and a member of a radical group known as the "Left Hegelians", and only gradually did he emerge from under the mantle of Hegel's thought. He developed from a partisan to a radical critic of Hegel, but in fact was never able to divorce himself totally from this powerful thinker's influence.

The beginner can discover quite adequately both the place of Hegel in the development of Western thought and a survey of his system by turning to any one of the standard encyclopedias in any library. The articles on Hegel are generally compiled by scholars and are recommended as first readings because they are so easily available. Especially recommended is the article, "Hegel," by T. M. Knox, in the *Encyclopedia Britannica*.

An equally rewarding source would be the chapter on Hegel in any good history of modern philosophy. Here the student will find biographical and bibliographical details, together with an overall view of Hegel's system and the influences on his thought. Some of the better and more competent of such studies are:

Mary W. Calkins: *The Persistant Problems of Philosophy* (New York, Macmillan, 1936, 601 pp.). Although this book was published in 1936, it is by no means outdated. It is a general history of modern philosophy but contains an excellent chapter on Hegel which includes biographical data and a careful analysis of his system. The author is herself a Hegelian.

James Collins: *A History of Modern European Philosophy* (Milwaukee, Bruce Publishing Co., 1954, 854 pp.). This is a standard history of modern philosophy. Chapter 14 is devoted to the study of Hegel and his philosophy. It begins with a presentation of the life and writings of Hegel, then discusses the influence of his predecessors on his thought and finally describes with careful analysis the whole system. At the end of the chapter on Hegel the student will find a neat summary and several pages of bibliography including both Hegel's own writings and other studies of this thinker up to the date of publication.

Frederick Copleston: *A History of Philosophy*, Vol. VII, *Fichte to Nietzsche* (Westminster, Md., The Newman Press, 1963, 8 vols.); Vol. VII, Part I, *Fichte to Hegel** (New York, Doubleday, 1965). Copleston has published this series covering the whole history of Western philosophy from the Greeks to the contemporary scene. His work is considered competent and a valuable aid for the undergraduate college student. The chapters on Hegel are rich in background material and relate Hegel's development to other philosophical movements that influenced his thought.

As the student advances he will undoubtedly desire a deeper understanding of Hegel's system. He can then turn to the following book-length studies.

Herbert Marcuse: *Reason and Revolution; Hegel and the Rise of Social Theory** (Boston, Beacon, 1966, 439 pp.). Part I presents the clearest analysis of Hegel's thought available in English and is perhaps the best source aside from the original texts of Hegel himself. It follows the development of Hegel's thought from the early theological writings through the first system, the logic, and finally the political philosophy and philosophy of history.

John N. Findlay: *Hegel, A Re-examination** (New York, Collier, 1962, 382 pp.). This book is an excellent introduction to Hegel by a philosopher who writes with an outspoken sympathy with Hegel's views. It includes a profound analysis of two of Hegel's key themes, the notion of spirit and the dialectical method, and a detailed presentation of the Hegelian system as found in two of Hegel's major works. The author appears as a devout Hegelian who exonerates the master from excessive subjectivity by showing that Hegel is describing the world as it really is. He gives the impression of fairness in his treatment and at the same time indicates that the so-called static concepts are relational notions always in the process of development according to the law of the dialectic.

Sydney Hook: *From Hegel to Marx** (Ann Arbor, Univ. of Michigan

Press, 1966, 335 pp.). The subtitle of this volume is: *Studies in the Intellectual Development of Karl Marx*. Hence it selects those aspects of Hegel's system that are pertinent to Marxism. Although only the first section is concerned with Hegel, the entire volume is valuable because of its treatment of the Young Hegelians, especially Feuerbach. The author, who was once a Marxist, is a scholar and the author of many books and articles. He does not probe deeply into the system but writes in a clear and interesting style. His own commitment to democracy appears throughout, and he emphasizes political philosophy rather than epistemological issues.

Walter Kaufmann: *Hegel, Reinterpretation, Texts and Commentary** (New York, Doubleday, 1965). An excellent introduction for the student of Hegel by a challenging contemporary professor at Princeton. It contains a brief biographical sketch of Hegel and a translation of the Preface to the *Phenomenology* with commentary on facing pages.

Karl Löwith: *From Hegel to Nietzsche, The Revolution in Nineteenth-Century Thought** (New York, Doubleday, 1967). An excellent study by a renowned student of Marxism.

R. G. Collingwood: *The Idea of Nature** (New York, Oxford Univ. Press, 1967). This work gives a brief account of the untranslated Part II of Hegel's *Encyclopedia of the Philosophical Sciences* and suggests some reasons for placing Hegel in the Aristotelian tradition. An enriching study by a thinker interested in the philosophy of history.

Finally, since there is no substitute for reading the actual texts of a philosopher, even though it has to be done in translation, the following works of Hegel, which are available in English and are important sources for Marx's philosophy, can be consulted:

G. F. W. Hegel: *Philosophy of Right** (trans. by T. M. Knox, Oxford, Oxford Univ. Press, 1967). This is one of the best places to begin reading the original works.

G. F. W. Hegel: *Lectures on the Philosophy of History** (trans. by J. Sibree, New York, Dover Publications, 1956). This edition contains a valuable introduction by Professor Carl Friedrich of Harvard University. But Hegel's own Introduction is considered by scholars to be one of the finest documents of Hegel's thought. Hence, if the student does no other reading of the original texts but this, he will be deeply rewarded. The work in general shows the fruitfulness of dialectic in its application to history. This work is also available in another paperback edition, *Reason in History** (trans. and ed. by Robert S. Hartman, New York, Library of Liberal Arts, 1953).

G. F. W. Hegel: *Philosophy of Mind* (trans. by W. Wallace from the *Encyclopedia of the Philosophical Sciences*, Oxford, Clarendon, 1894). This is one of the works published by Hegel himself and is still considered a good place for the beginning student to start.

G. F. W. Hegel: *Logic* (trans. by W. Wallace from the *Encyclopedia of the Philosophical Sciences*, Oxford, Clarendon, 1968). This is far better than the following as an introduction to logic.

G. F. W. Hegel: *Science of Logic* (trans. by W. H. Johnston and L. G. Struthers, 2 vols., New York, Macmillan, 1961). A rather unwieldly volume not recommended, because of its difficulty for the beginning student of Marxism.

G. F. W. Hegel: *Phenomenology of Mind** (trans. by J. B. Bailie, New York, Harper and Row, 1967). This is often considered Hegel's most important work, and it is the one most often referred to. However, it is extremely difficult. It is suggested that the beginner turn to the index at the end of this edition and select some key Hegelian idea such as the "Absolute" and then read the pertinent passages given as references. In this way the student will not try to read the entire work but may find his interest growing beyond the selected passages; at any rate he will be deeply rewarded by perusing the text itself. The translation by Baillie is considered faithful and competent. The introduction to this particular edition was written by George Lichtheim, who is a recognized Marxist scholar.

G. F. W. Hegel: *Lectures on the History of Philosophy* (trans. by E. S. Haldane and F. H. Simson, 3 volumes, New York, Humanities Press, 1955). These lectures were first published in English in London in 1892 and they mark the beginning of the study of the history of philosophical ideas in the modern sense. Not recommended as essential for the beginner.

Ludwig Feuerbach

Ludwig Feuerbach (1804-1872) is, among the Left Hegelians, the thinker who most influenced Marx (as well as Engels) in his early development. Feuerbach's materialist critique of Hegel made possible Marx's own rejection of Hegelian idealism and the formulation of a kind of naturalist humanism. Further, Feuerbach's critique of religion—for which he is most widely known—was enthusiastically adopted by Marx, and provided the germ from which certain important principles of historical materialism were to grow. Engels himself recognized the debt that he and Marx owed to this thinker, who, Engels says, "forms an intermediate link between Hegelian philosophy and our conception."

The best place for the beginning student to obtain some knowledge of Feuerbach is the article on him in the *Encyclopedia Britannica*; if the 1901 edition is available, it is to be preferred, since the article here is more extensive. For a more thorough knowledge of Feuerbach's position, the student could first turn to the above-mentioned books by Sidney Hook (*From Hegel to Marx*) and Herbert Marcuse (*Reason and Revolution*). The seventh chapter of Hook's study treats Feuerbach in a competent and scholarly fashion. Marcuse sketches very briefly the way in which Feuerbach mediates the transition from Hegel to Marx. The following books are recommended for further study:

Robert Tucker: *Philosophy and Myth in Karl Marx** (Cambridge, University Press, 1969). This is the best philosophical treatment in English of Feuerbach in relation to Marxism. The tone is scholarly, the treatment adequate, and the whole volume should be read by the student interested in Marxism.

Karl Löwith: *From Hegel to Nietzsche, The Revolution in Nineteenth-Century Thought** (New York, Doubleday, 1967). A prominent German student of Marxism here presents a section describing the influence of Feuerbach on the young Marx.

William Chamberlain: *Heaven Wasn't His Destination: The Philosophy of Ludwig Feuerbach* (London, G. Allen and Unwin, 1941). This is the best exposition of Feuerbach's life and thought in English to date. Since there is no standard biography of Feuerbach in either German or English, this book is recommended because of its rich background material.

The student of Marxism may not at first be able to spend much time on Feuerbach; thus, before some of Feuerbach's own writings are mentioned, it is appropriate to point to a work about him by Friedrich Engels, Marx's collaborator and frequent co-author. This short work represents the standard Marxist evaluation of the importance of Feuerbach:

Friedrich Engels: *Ludwig Feuerbach and the Outcome of Classical German Philosophy** (New York, International Publishers, 1941). There are several English editions of this work by Engels which is more of a general presentation of Marxist philosophy than a study of Feuerbach. But Engels does consider here the importance and influence of Feuerbach in relation to the formation of Marx's and Engel's views. There is an appendix containing the famous "Theses on Feuerbach," written by Marx himself.

Some works of Feuerbach are available in English:

Ludwig Feuerbach: *The Essence of Christianity** (New York, Harper and Row, 1957). This is Feuerbach's most famous work. It attacks Christianity as an abstract ideal wherein God is not a real entity. This theme comes from Feuerbach's rejection of Hegel's idea of the Absolute.

Ludwig Feuerbach: *The Essence of Christianity** (trans. by George

Eliot, Part I, the entire text; Part II, edited and condensed by F. W. Strothmann and E. Graham Waring, New York, P. Ungar Publishing Company, 1957). Part II is especially recommended. This is another edition of the above. Strothmann and Waring have incorporated in their abridgment of this text all the important sections for the serious undergraduate student of Marxism.

Ludwig Feuerbach: *Lectures on the Essence of Religion* (New York, Harper and Row, 1967). Again we perceive the new interest in Feuerbach with the publication of his lectures given at Heidelburg University in 1848-49. These lectures are a fuller development of the briefer work simply entitled, *The Essence of Religion* (1845), and represent Feuerbach's contribution to the revolutionary activity of that year. In this work he expands his attack against all religion rather than confining his criticism to Christianity.

Ludwig Feuerbach: *The Essence of Faith According to Luther* (trans. by Melvin Cherno, New York, Harper and Row, 1967). The introduction to Cherno's translation is especially worthwhile in enabling the reader readily to grasp the milieu in which Feuerbach was working and thinking. However, the work itself is of more value for a student of theology.

Ludwig Feuerbach: *Philosophy of the Future** (New York, Library of the Liberal Arts, 1966). It is interesting that this rather obscure treatise of Feuerbach has been published so recently in English. In this work, Feuerbach explains his notion of sensual existence, i.e., the priority of the sentient individual in all philosophical considerations.

3
KARL MARX

Karl Marx (1818-1883) inspired the development of Marxism and of Marxism-Leninism. Hegel and the Young Hegelians, specifically, and German Idealism, generally, were major influences, but not the only ones, on Marx's thought. The French socialists and the English economists were significant in determining the direction of his later development, and their influence becomes more visible than the Hegelian one in his later writings. His last major work published during his life, *Capital* (Vol. I), is not intended as a philosophical work, but rather as a critique of capitalist economy. Indeed it is held by some scholars that there is a radical split between Marx the young Hegelian, and Marx the mature scientific socialist. But most scholars of Marxian thought believe there to be a continuity between the young and old Marx. The works of the young Marx lay the philosophical foundations implicit in the late economic works. Whichever side of the argument one chooses to follow, one point will remain the same: Marx did write some works that are quite definitely philosophical, others that can be considered as transitions from theory to application, and finally some works that are not philosophical at all. Our interest here is primarily with the philosophical works and how the student might best approach them.

One should first put himself into the Marxian framework. Three readings will prove helpful in beginning one's study of Marx:

Neil McInnes: "Karl Marx," in *The Encyclopedia of Philosophy*, Vol. V. (New York, The Macmillan Company and The Free Press, 1967, pp. 171-173). This article contains the essential biographical

22

material on Marx. Most other encyclopedia articles on Marx will present the same information.

More important than biographical information are certain fundamental themes in Marx's work that need to be recognized initially. These themes are treated in:

Robert W. Daniels: "Marxism," in *The Encyclopedia Americana*, Vol. XVIII (New York, Americana Corporation, 1969, pp. 345a-345h). This article is possibly the most comprehensive encyclopedia article in English on Marxism. The first part of it is devoted to a concise, lucid statement of Marxian themes while the final sections are devoted to the different transformations made in these themes by Lenin and Stalin. Critical remarks are included.

Since it is impossible to understand Marx's position without some knowledge of the general cultural background and the currents of thought which influenced him, the student would do well to take up the following book, which also presents a clear introduction to Marx's main themes:

Isaiah Berlin: *Karl Marx, His Life and Environment** (New York, Oxford Univ. Press, 1968, 295 pp.). This well written and readily available biography discusses Marx's intellectual development against the background of German philosophy, French socialism, and English political economy. It considers the life of Marx in his physical and intellectual surroundings and treats his thoughts as the integral part of his life that they were.

After the student has oriented himself in this way, he should turn to Marx's works themselves. *The Economic and Philosophical Manuscripts of 1844* offers an excellent starting point for beginning a study of Marx. These manuscripts, which were not published until 1932, fifty years after Marx's death, have given rise to controversial discussions concerning the humanism of Marx and have awakened new hopes in some Marxist and Christian scholars for dialogue between the two groups. The impact of these manuscripts is felt very strongly in the East European countries, where schools of Neo-Marxist philosophy emphasizing themes such as alienation, freedom, and responsibility have developed. In the United States, the *Manuscripts* have only been available for widespread use since the publication of Erich Fromm's *Marx's Concept of Man* in 1960. Since that time they have increased considerably in importance in discussions of Marxism. Thus if the student wants a critical understanding of much of the discussion about Marxism today, a comprehension of these manuscripts is indispensible.

The *Manuscripts* have been published in several English translations, but one of the most worthwhile for study is:

Karl Marx: *The Economic and Philosophic Manuscripts of 1844** (ed. and intro. by Dirk J. Struik, New York, International Publishers, 1964, 255 pp.). Professor Struik analyzes the *Manuscripts*, discusses their biographical-philosophical background, and examines some of their major themes. He is careful to point out some of the pitfalls in studying the *Manuscripts* and some basic misinterpretations that have arisen since their publication.

One edition of the *Manuscripts*, which includes an important commentary, is:

Erich Fromm: *Marx's Concept of Man** (New York, Ungar, 1969, 263 pp.). It was in this book that sections of T. B. Bottomore's translation of the *Manuscripts* were first published in the United States. Fromm's book excludes the parts of the *Manuscripts* on economics and society and does not comment on them. The result is an overemphasis on the alienation theme. This failing can be compensated by reading the introduction in the Struik edition just mentioned. The value of Fromm's work should not be underrated however. It is a good book for use in dispelling many popular misconceptions about Marx's thought.

When the *Manuscripts* have been digested by the student, he may wish to move to other philosophical works by Marx. There are two works which can advantageously be used together:

Lloyd D. Easton and Kurt H. Guddat: *Writings of the Young Marx on Philosophy and Society** (New York, Doubleday, 1967, 506 pp.). This is an anthology of the most important of Marx's early philosophical writings.

Louis Dupré: *The Philosophical Foundations of Marxism** (New York, Harcourt, Brace and World, 1966, 240 pp.). Dupré gives an analysis of the development of Hegel's thought and its transformation through the Young Hegelians to Marx. Marx's philosophical writings and their development through *The Poverty of Philosophy* and *The Communist Manifesto* are examined with a view to establishing those philosophical premises which are operative in the later economic and social works. *The Poverty of Philosophy* and *The Communist Manifesto* are seen as transition works from theory to application. By studying the appropriate selections in the anthology of Easton and Guddat (*The Communist Manifesto* is not contained in this anthology. See below for available editions.), and then turning to the examinations presented by Dupré, the student can assure himself of a firm foundation for further study of Marx.

There are many editions of Marx's writings, both in single editions and in selected works, which are readily available. The Easton and Guddat edition is the most useful. Marx was constantly developing his major ideas throughout his writing career. It is possible to follow the development of one or two of Marx's major themes by judiciously using the index in the Easton and Guddat edition or in the other works. However, if the student wants to be seriously conversant in Marx's thought he should work carefully through Marx's major writings. A chronological overview is available in:

T. B. Bottomore (ed. and trans.) and Maximilien Rubel (ed.): *Karl Marx, Selected Writings in Sociology and Social Philosophy** (New York, McGraw-Hill, 1964, 268 pp., cf. pp. 259-264). This selection of Marx's works contains, besides the excerpts, a helpful bibliography, which "lists Marx's principal writings in chronological order, with the dates of original publication and of the main English translations."

Marx's main writings should be read in the order in which he wrote them. For example:

> Karl Marx: *The Difference Between the Democritean and Epicurean Philosophy of Nature*, in *Activity in Marx's Philosophy* by Norman Livergood (The Hague, Martinus Nijhoff, 1967, 109 pp.). This is Norman Livergood's translation of the dissertation which won Marx a Ph.D. from the University of Jena in April 1841. This dissertation was first published only in 1932. Marx here compares two early Greek materialist philosophers, Democritus and Epicurus, and the results of this study can be seen in the development of Marx's own concept of materialism. Marx's strong anthropocentric view shows itself clearly in his tribute to Prometheus, who Marx believes "is the most eminent saint and martyr in the philosophic calendar." Livergood presents in the first half of the book a discussion of the notion of activity as it relates to Marx's materialism, epistemology, and philosophy. Livergood's work is especially helpful in exploring the way Marx's dissertation relates to his later works.

On the Jewish Question and *Contribution to the Critique of Hegel's Philosophy of Right* should be examined next. They were both written at the end of 1843 and published in the *Deutsch-Französische Jahrbücher* in February of 1844. *The Economic and Philosophical Manuscripts* was written during the summer of 1844 in Paris. As has already been mentioned, they were not published until 1932, as was also the case with Marx's Ph.D. dissertation described above; this means that the first generation of Marxists did not have access to an extremely important period in Marx's intellectual development. These three works are contained in:

> Karl Marx: *Early Writings** (edited by T. B. Bottomore, New York, McGraw-Hill, 1963, 227 pp.). In *On the Jewish Question*, Marx argues that exclusively political emancipation is incomplete without the emancipation of man in his everyday life and work. The philosophical implications of this insight are profound and should be carefully pondered by the student. In this light, special consideration needs to be given to the whole notion of political power. The

Contribution to the Critique of Hegel's Philosophy of Right presents a strong attack on Hegel's speculative philosophy, though it preserves the notion of the dialectical movement of history. Marx, under the influence of the French socialists, claims that the proletariat, the most alienated class, will provide the means to break the chains of bourgeois society. The proletariat is the mover of history, contrary to Hegel's claim. Is this role really that of the proletariat, or has the dialectic created a false sense of optimism? The contemporary discussion of a worker-student alliance would indicate that this issue is far from dead. *The Economic and Philosophical Manuscripts* offers very important discussions of the nature of labor, alienation, and money. Likewise one should study carefully Marx's critique of Hegel, and in particular the notion of labor as a self-creative process. Note that Marx is very conscious of the impact of external conditions in either making possible or obviating the possibility of one's self-development through work. This raises the important question of how society might be arranged to allow for man's full human development. This Bottomore edition includes a helpful subject index, which the earlier cited Dirk Struik edition of *Manuscripts* lacks; however, the latter is valuable in working through these and other important questions, because of its introduction and carefully prepared notes.

Karl Marx: *The Holy Family* (trans. by R. Dixon, Moscow, Foreign Languages Publishing House, 1956, 299 pp.). Marx, with some assistance from Engels, finished this work in November 1844 and published it in February 1845. Compared to the *Manuscripts*, this work proves to be more polemical than profound.

The next major step in Marx's intellectual development was taken in *The German Ideology*:

Karl Marx and Friedrich Engels: *The German Ideology** (Parts I and III, edited with an introduction by R. Pascal, New York, International Publishers, 1965). In February 1845 Marx was expelled from France. He settled in Brussels, where he and Engels worked on their first major joint project. *The German Ideology* was first published only in 1932 along with the *Manuscripts*, thus ushering in a new era in Marxian scholarship. The first part of the work deserves careful reading because of its importance in the development of Marx's understanding of the role of ideology.

Karl Marx: *The Poverty of Philosophy** (with an intro. by F. Engels, New York, International Publishers, 1969, 233 pp.). This work was written in the spring of 1847 and published in the same year. Writing in response to Pierre Joseph Proudhon's *Philosophy of Poverty*, Marx argues that Proudhon did not see the historical interconnection between social relations and the forces of production. Marx maintains that men produce not only linen, flax, etc., but also social relations in conformity with their material productivity.

Karl Marx and Friedrich Engels: The Communist Manifesto* (New York, Washington Square Press, 1970, 158 pp., and numerous other editions). Having written about the role of the proletariat, Marx and Engels now call them to action. The *Manifesto* is often the only work of Marx read, yet without an understanding of Marx's earlier works it is easily misunderstood.

Karl Marx: *Pre-Capitalist Economic Formations** (trans. by Jack Cohen, edited with an intro. by E. J. Hobsbown, New York, International Publishers, 1966, 153 pp.). This is a translation of a section of Marx's *Grundrisse* written in 1857-58, which has caused a further re-evaluation of Marx's thought, especially since the German edition of 1953 has given it a wider audience. Eric Hobsbown, who has contributed a very helpful introduction to the work, writes, "It can be said without hesitation that any Marxist historical discussion which does not take into account the present work . . . must be reconsidered in its light." Here is another indication, along with the work of the younger Marx, that there is still much room for creative Marxian scholarship which may well save Marx from a dogmatization of his thoughts.

Karl Marx: *A Contribution to the Critique of Political Economy** (New York, International Publishers, 1970, 264 pp.). This work is of less direct philosophical interest and indicates Marx's transition to a serious consideration of economics. It was written in 1859.

Karl Marx: *Capital, A Critique of Political Economy** (New York, International Publishers, 1967, 3 vols.). Marx's major work, the first volume of which was published in 1867, is a significant contribution to economic theory. In preparing it, Marx spent more hours in the library of the British Museum than on the barricades of the revolution. Read in recent years in the light of Marx's earlier works it has taken on a new significance. Marx concentrates on the problem of exploitation and its causes rather than on alienation. Nevertheless, many contemporary scholars have turned back to the concept of alienation as a richer and more complex concept in order to explain the problems inherent in the concept of exploitation. *Capital* should be read selectively after Marx's other material has been carefully studied.

There are a number of selected and specialized collections which we can only mention:

Karl Marx and Friedrich Engels: *Selected Works** (New York, International Publishers, 1968, 800 pp.).

Marx and Engels Basic Writings on Politics and Philosophy* (edited by Lewis Feuer, New York, Doubleday, 1959, 497 pp.). This work does not include the *Manuscripts*.

Karl Marx, *et al.: The Woman Question** (New York, International Publishers, 1970, 96 pp.).

In terms of Marxian scholarship there are two standard reference works which are often mentioned, *Marx-Engels Gesamtausgabe* (MEGA), and *Marx-Engels Werke* (MEW). They are both in German and therefore probably inaccessible for most beginning students. However, it is important that one know of their existence, especially because there is no complete edition of Marx in English:

Karl Marx and Friedrich Engels: *Historisch-kritische Gesamtausgabe*, (MEGA) (5 vols., edited by D. Rjazanov and V. Adoratski, Berlin, Marx-Engels Verlag, 1927-1932).

Karl Marx and Friedrich Engels: *Karl Marx, Friedrich Engels, Werke*, (MEW) (39 vols., Berlin, Dietz, 1960-1969).

A serious study of Marx includes not only familiarity with Marx's works themselves, but also a knowledgeable acquaintance with the important secondary literature. Remember that Marx came out of a different philosophical tradition than most English speaking students do. In order to break out of our empirical tradition, a great deal of hard, concentrated effort is necessary, especially because the terminology and "flow of thought" of Marx are much different from ours. For example, implied in the notion of alienation as used by Marx is an understanding of a larger process which will enable alienation to be transcended. "Alienation" as used in our Anglo-Saxon world does not usually include a realization that it is part of a larger process of dialectical development. Some of these difficulties will be clarified when one reads the excellent secondary sources now available in English.

We will concentrate on those works of particular philosophical significance. Most of the works trace Hegel's and Feuerbach's influence on Marx and go on to discuss his early writings with particular emphasis on his notions of alienation and labor. Most scholars argue for a general continuity in the development of Marx's thought between the early and later works: these include Tucker, Struik, Schaff, Petrovic, Fromm, and many others. The notable exceptions are Althusser and Feuer.

The following works make significant contributions towards the interpretation of Marx's thought:

Robert Tucker: *Philosophy and Myth in Karl Marx** (New York, Cambridge Univ. Press, 1967, 263 pp.). This is an excellent place to start. Tucker re-evaluates Marx on the basis of his earlier works and pays particular attention to the notion of alienation. He traces carefully Marx's inverting of Hegel's Objective Spirit. He argues that Marx was more a moralist than an economist, and that a "mythical" vision is the basis upon which Marx's ideational superstructure is built.

Roger Garaudy: *Karl Marx, The Evolution of His Thought** (trans. by Nan Aptheker, New York, International Publishers, 1967, 223 pp.). This offers a valuable contrast to Tucker's philosophical study of Marx. Garaudy writes with the flare of a passionate but intelligent Marxist-Leninist. He sees Marx, not Kant, as effecting the true "Copernican" revolution in philosophy: "In placing man and his struggles at the center of the world rather than regarding man as an abstract 'subject,' in making philosophy come down from heaven to earth and observe the toil and the struggles of men, Marxism became an active force."

Shlomo Avineri: *The Social and Political Thought of Karl Marx* (Cambridge, Cambridge Univ. Press, 1969, 258 pp.). Avineri offers an examination of the major concepts in Marx's writing in light of the early writings, supporting the thesis of the continuity of Marx's thought. He includes sections on Marx's relation to Hegel and Feuerbach and sections on The Paris Commune and the stages of socialism. This is a significant contribution to the study of Marxian thought.

Sidney Hook: *From Hegel to Marx, Studies in the Intellectual Development of Karl Marx** (Ann Arbor, Univ. of Michigan Press, 1968, 335 pp.). This is one of the very best studies on the philosophical background of Marx. Sidney Hook discusses the influences of Hegel, Strauss, Bauer, Ruge, Stirner, Hess, and Feuerbach on Marx. He also includes an important discussion and explanation of Marx's *Theses on Feuerbach*.

Robert Tucker: *The Marxian Revolutionary Idea** (New York, Norton, 1970, 240 pp.). This is a sequel to Tucker's previous work. Assuming the unity in Marx, Tucker discusses the notions of revolution, ethics, state, politics, and the Marxian contribution to the modernization process. This work should be studied after working carefully through Tucker's first book as well as through Hook's and others.

Louis Althusser: *For Marx** (New York, Random, 1970, 247 pp.). Althusser argues for a separation between the young and the old Marx. His central point is the claim that an "epistemological break" occurred around the time of the *German Ideology* (1845) which separates the humanistic and still ideological speculations of the young Marx from the mature elaboration of historical materialism.

Karl Löwith: *From Hegel to Nietzsche, The Revolution in Nineteenth-Century Thought** (New York, Doubleday, 1967). This work contains excellent discussions of the problems of work, education, and man, and is particularly significant for its development of the notion of work through the thought of Hegel, Marx, Kierkegaard, and Nietzsche. This is helpful in putting Marx in a broader philosophical context, because it is important to remember that Marx is not the beginning and end of philosophy; rather, he works very much within our Western philosophical tradition.

Henry J. Koren: *Marx and the Authentic Man, A First Introduction to the Philosophy of Karl Marx* (Pittsburgh, Duquesne Univ. Press, 1967, 150 pp.). For a student who has had little exposure to philosophical thought, this offers a relatively easy approach to Marx. It is written primarily for beginners. Koren begins with a biographical sketch of Marx, mentions the influences on him, discusses Marx's central notion of man as a "self-realizing being" in the work process, how man is estranged under capitalism, and how the Communist society has promised the transcendence of alienation, while the Soviet regime has perpetrated the "inauthentic man."

Raya Dunayevskaya: *Marxism and Freedom . . . From 1776 Until*

Today (preface by H. Marcuse, New York, Bookman Associates, 1958, 384 pp.). Coming from a Russian who is sympathetic to Marx, the attack on the Soviet position in Chapter III is of real interest. She finds that the Soviet attack on Marx's *Economic and Philosophical Manuscripts* "continues to spend incredible time and energy and vigilance to imprison Marx within the bounds of the private property versus State property concept." It has only been in the last few years that the Soviets and East Germans have added Marx's *Manuscripts* to their collections of his works. For many years they chose to ignore the significance of this work, maintaining that it did not reflect the work of the mature Marx.

Nicholas Lobkowicz: *Theory and Practice, History of a Concept from Aristotle to Marx* (Notre Dame, Univ. of Notre Dame Press, 1967, 442 pp.). This is a highly significant study for the field of Marxian scholarship. Lobkowicz has a couple of really excellent chapters on the notions of labor and praxis in Marx. This work is highly recommended for the student who wants to deepen his understanding of the Marxian tradition.

Karl R. Popper: *High Tide of Prophecy, Hegel, Marx, and the Aftermath*, Vol. II of *The Open Society and Its Enemies** (New York, Harper and Row, 1963, 391 pp.). Karl Popper, a leading neo-positivist in social theory, offers one of the most substantial philosophical refutations of Marx from the Western side. While admitting the humanitarian impulse in Marx's thought, he claims his "attempt to apply rational methods to the most urgent problems of social life" has been unsuccessful. There is no such thing as a "concrete history of mankind." Thus attempts to justify acts on the basis of the meaning of history are futile. History has no meaning and it is here that Marx fails.

Marx's thought has been interwoven with that of Engels, Plekhanov, Lenin, Stalin, and others. Marx is commonly and incorrectly referred to as a "dialectical materialist." In order to disengage Marx's original contribution from the later "Marxisms" one may wish to refer to:

Z. A. Jordan, *The Evolution of Dialectical Materialism, A Philosophical and Sociological Analysis.* (New York: St. Martin's Press, 1967, 490 pp.). Jordan carefully unwinds Marx's anthropological naturalism from the thought of Engels, Plekhanov, Lenin, and Stalin. In turn he traces the philosophical sources and revisions of dialectical materialism and discusses the connections between dialectical and historical materialism.

The student who in the course of his study wishes to investigate more thoroughly the connections between the events of Marx's life and the development of his thought may turn to the following biographies:

Franz Mehring: *Karl Marx, The Story of His Life** (Ann Arbor, Univ. of Michigan Press, 1969, 575 pp.). Mehring's biography was originally published in German in 1918. It has become the classic biography of Marx, but it should be noted that Mehring makes no claim of coming to grips with the thought of Marx, although Marx's background is discussed thoroughly and the influences on him are examined.

John Lewis: *The Life and Teachings of Karl Marx** (New York, International Publishers, 1965, 286 pp.). Of special interest in this biography are the evaluations of Marx as economist and historian, and the discussion of Marx's relation to various political movements and the states existing during his life.

For those students who are interested in continuing their study of Marx, access to a good bibliography of his work is necessary. *Marxist Philosophy, A Bibliographical Guide* (Chapel Hill, Univ. of North Carolina Press, 1967) by John Lachs has already been mentioned in the Introduction, but deserves to be mentioned again, because it is the most complete bibliography of studies on Marx in English. If Lach's work is unavailable, many books on Marx contain bibliographies that are helpful. For the student who reads French, it must be noted that Maximilien Rubel's *Bibliographie des Oeuvres de Karl Marx** (Paris, Librairie Marcel Rivière et Cie, 1956, 272 pp.) is a complete and annotated bibliography of Marx's published works.

4

GERMAN CLASSICAL MARXISM

Friedrich Engels

Friedrich Engels (1820-1895) was the closest friend, collaborator, and benefactor of Karl Marx. In the development of the philosophy of Marxism, the contributions of Engels are essential. Not only did he co-author several works with Marx, write the introductions to others, and edit and publish the second and third volumes of *Capital* after Marx's death, but his own writings extend the Marxist concepts of materialism and dialectics beyond the socioeconomic and historical applications that Marx had given them. In effect, Engels presents an all-inclusive world view in which nearly every sphere of traditional philosophical analysis is interpreted through the concepts of materialism and dialectics. In attempting to present a total philosophical system, he developed the philosophy of Classical Marxism which we know by the name *Dialectical Materialism*.

Since the philosophy of any man is very much influenced by his intellectual and cultural milieu, the first step toward understanding him must be the study of his life and times. For the purposes of the beginning student, a perusal of the life and works of Engels as presented in any available encyclopedia is valuable. See, for example:

> *The International Encyclopedia of the Social Sciences* (New York, Macmillan, 1968, vol. 5, pp. 64-69). The biography of Engels in this book is a good one with a sociological orientation.

It would be advisable for the student of philosophy to read the study of Engels as presented by a good history of philosophy. The lives and works of Marx and Engels are closely intertwined, and most historians of philosophy treat them together. See, for example, these two books; the first is better for introductory purposes:

A. James Gregor: *A Survey of Marxism* (New York, Random House, 1965, 370 pp.). This book presents a survey of the philosophy of Marxism-Leninism as it developed from the works of Marx, Engels, and Lenin. Each man is presented in turn with a good short biography followed by a study of his intellectual development and of his contribution to the philosophical system. The second chapter deals with the life and thought of Engels.

Frederick Copleston: *A History of Philosophy** (New York, Doubleday, 1965, 276 pp. vol. VII, Part II, pp. 73-104). One of the best histories of philosophy available in English, this book provides the student with a good short introduction to the lives, works and thought of Marx and Engels. However, the biography of Engels comprises only one paragraph, presenting his essential background before he met Marx. The rest of the chapter treats the lives and thought of the two men together.

With an appreciation of the life and times of the man, and some basic understanding of his thought, one should proceed to Engels' works. A good general introductory text is Gregor's *A Survey of Marxism*, cited above, or:

Richard T. DeGeorge: *Patterns of Soviet Thought* (Ann Arbor, Univ. of Michigan Press, 1966, 293 pp.). This volume traces the development of Marxist-Leninist philosophy from its foundations in the thought of Marx and Engels and concludes with some of the problems of contemporary Soviet interpretation. In chapter 5, the author gives a short biography of Engels, placing him in the context of Marxist thought. He then gives a summary of Engels' *Anti-Dühring*, *Ludwig Feuerbach*, and *The Dialectics of Nature*, with an evaluation of Engel's contribution to Soviet thought, and a short discussion of the "Orthodox" and "Revisionist" interpretations of Classical Marxism.

Although books that survey the life and thought of a man have the value of introducing and orienting the student of his philosophy, the serious student must read at least some of the original works in their complete form. The writings of Engels can be divided into those which he co-authored with Marx and those of which he is the sole or principal author. Those in which he collaborated with Marx are:

Karl Marx and Friedrich Engels: *The Communist Manifesto** (New York, International Publishers, 1948). Though not a philosophical treatise, the *Manifesto* is important for its impact and for its presentation of the fundamental concepts of the Marxist world view.

Karl Marx and Friedrich Engels: *The Holy Family* (Moscow, Foreign Languages Publishing House, 1956, 299 pp.). Although primarily the work of Marx, Engels cooperated in this polemic against the Bauer brothers and their followers, members of the Hegelian Right who emphasized the value of the individual in changing history. To the contrary, Marx and Engels assert that the mass, the class, changes history, not individuals. The fundamental philosophical concepts expressed are the value of the impersonal class as a moving force in history, the inevitability of Communism (historical determinism), and materialism.

Karl Marx and Friedrich Engels: *The German Ideology* (New York, International Publishers, 1942). Written in 1846, this work contains the earliest statement of the materialist interpretation of history with the relationship of man's intellectual activity to the economic base.

Some of the works of Engels himself are:

Friedrich Engels: *Ludwig Feuerbach and the Outcome of Classical*

*German Philosophy** (New York, International Publishers, 1941). If a student were to choose only one of Engel's works, this is the one he should read in its entirety. It traces the development of his theory from Hegel to the materialism of Feuerbach, finally culminating in dialectical materialism. In the four parts of the book, Engels presents his analysis of the disputes between the Hegelian Right and the Hegelian Left, the concepts of idealism and materialism (the classical definitions of which almost all subsequent Marxists have adopted), his criticism of Feuerbach's theories on religion and ethics, and finally, applying the concept of the dialectic to nature and history, the classical theories of dialectical materialism and historical materialism.

Friedrich Engels: *Anti-Dühring, Herr Eugen Dühring's Revolution in Science** (New York, International Publishers, 1959, 542 pp.). Responding to Dühring's attempt to reform the theory of socialism, Engels applies the concept of the dialectic to natural science and mathematics, producing, albeit in polemic form, the first systematic presentation of the philosophy of dialectical materialism. Accusing Dühring of being guilty of idealism, he first presents the materialistic theory of knowledge—that concepts are created by objective reality, not the inverse—and therefore rejects Dühring's implication that the theories of man should change the world. In view of this dialectical and materialistic theory of knowledge, Engels then discusses the philosophical concepts of time and space, matter and motion, evolution with dialectical leaps from quantity to quality, the relativity of truth and morality, and freedom and necessity.

Friedrich Engels: *Dialectics of Nature** (New York, International Publishers, 1964, 407 pp.). Whereas in *Anti-Dühring*, Engels attempts a systematic response to Dühring's philosophical system, his presentation lacks the impersonal and objective attitude which should characterize every scientific effort. His *Dialectics of Nature*, the result of many years of independent study of science and mathematics, is an attempt to present generally the same theories in an objective and scientific manner. Trying to reconcile the philosophy of materialism with experimental science, Engels offers the dialectic as the only proper method of investigation of all scientific disciplines. Here he articulates his classic three laws of the dialectic. It must be noted that this book was not published until 1925, after the death of Lenin. Thus, Lenin did not have the opportunity to use it in his interpretation of Marxism.

Friedrich Engels: *Socialism, Utopian and Scientific** (New York, International Publishers, 1968). This pamphlet was composed from three chapters of *Anti-Dühring* and published in 1880. It more briefly presents Engels' criticism of all preceeding socialist theories as unrealistic and utopian and contrasts them to dialectical materialism, which he describes as the only truly scientific socialism. The systems of socialism presented by the likes of Saint-Simon, Fourier, and Owen are utopian because they were articulated before capitalism had objectively developed enough to be evaluated correctly. Dialectics, on the other hand, develops with objective conditions and can accurately evaluate and cope with capitalism, leading finally to the withering away of the state and the advent of freedom.

Friedrich Engels: *The Origin of the Family, Private Property, and the State** (New York, International Publishers, 1935, 217 pp.). As the title implies, Engels traces the development of the institutions of family, private property, and the state as products of historically evolving economic and material conditions. As the means of production and productive relations evolved throughout history, the state and all of its legal structures were produced as weapons of suppression by the ruling classes over the oppressed classes. With the increase of class tension to the point of revolution, socialism will emerge, with the concurrent elimination of all classes. Therefore, the state will wither away with all of its appurtenances, giving way to true freedom.

Among the secondary literature, two special works can be recommended for the student who wishes to pursue further his study of Engels:

Gustav Mayer: *Friedrich Engels, a Biography* (edited by R. H. S.

Crossman, New York, H. Fertig, 1969, 332 pp.). This is the classic biography of Engels and the only adequate one in English.

Gustav Wetter: *Dialectical Materialism** (New York, Praeger, 1958, 609 pp.). This is an in-depth study presenting a historical and systematic survey of Marxist-Leninist philosophy from its genesis in Hegel to contemporary Soviet philosophy up to 1956. It shows, among other things, the development of the thought of Engels taken over by the Soviets. This book, founded upon original sources and enriched with a copious bibliography of the literature available to the date of publication, has a philosophical depth that makes it a classic, but which also makes it rather difficult for the beginner. It remains one of the standard works in the field.

The Classical Marxists

Even before the death of Marx in 1885, intense discussion began as to the best manner to implement his theories. Mass parties of working men in Europe were led by middle-class intellectuals to adopt his theories as the guide to their economic and political struggles. The German Social-Democratic Party was the most influential of these, but there were Marxist parties in France and England as well. Russian Marxism was represented primarily by those intellectuals who had fled the oppressive measures of the Czar and were living in voluntary or forced exile in Europe. The complexities of Marxist theories demanded interpretation to be accommodated to the practical problems of the different countries and of the changing conditions of the working man. The primary interpretations which arose can be classified by the terms Orthodox Marxists and Revisionists. For a general introduction to the question of Orthodox versus Revisionist men and views, consult Richard DeGeorge's *Patterns of Soviet Thought*, as cited above, pp. 108-111, or:

Sidney Hook: *Marx and the Marxists, The Ambiguous Legacy** (New York, Van Nostrand, 1955, 245 pp.). Hook presents a short introductory study of the thoughts of Marx and some of the most important orthodox and revisionist followers of Marx. The second part of the book presents a brief anthology of pertinent quotations from the persons cited in the text.

The orthodox Marxists were led by Engels himself until his death in 1895, then by the chief theoretician of the German Social-Democratic Party, Karl Kautsky, and by the Russian exile George Plekhanov. The term "orthodox" in this context must not be interpreted in light of subsequent Leninist and Soviet developments, for many and grave differences exist between them. Concerning those later developments, see the next chapter, "Soviet Marxism-Leninism." The orthodox Marxists attempted to preserve the purity of the thought of Marx and Engels. They emphasized the concepts of materialism, the dialectic, evolutionary historical determinism, democratic socialism, and the systematic unity of Marx and Engels.

Karl Kautsky (1854-1938) was the stolid and conscientious defender of the original theory of Marx and Engels. Emphasizing historical determinism, he deplored revolutionary impatience which would impose the socialist dream and encouraged a slow and patient cooperation with the development of the socioeconomic conditions of evolving history. Among his works, the student would be well advised to read one of the following:

Karl Kautsky: *The Dictatorship of the Proletariat** (Ann Arbor, Univ. of Michigan Press, 1964, 149 pp.). Although an orthodox defense of Marxism, this book expresses criticism of Lenin's theories of the part played by the proletariat in the revolution. For Kautsky, the Party is a revolutionary party, not a revolution-making party, and Lenin's idea of the Party as the vanguard of the proletariat was anathema to his Social-Democratic convictions.

Karl Kautsky: *Ethics and the Materialistic Conception of History* (Chicago, Charles H. Kerr, 1907, trans. by H. J. Stenning). This is Kautsky's defense of historical materialism with emphasis upon the economic substructure as the ultimate determinant of society and its development in history.

George Plekhanov (1856-1918) was one of the Russian emigres who had taken refuge in Europe, especially in Switzerland. Specializing in the defense of Marxist orthodoxy against its critics, he emphasized a monistic world view that was in accord with Marx as developed by Engels; his first intention was to implement these theories in Russia. For the life and times of George Plekhanov read:

Samuel Baron: *Plekhanov, The Father of Russian Revolution* (Stanford, Stanford Univ. Press, 1963, 400 pp.). This is the first and only biography of Plekhanov in English.

Among his works the student should be familiar with:

George Plekhanov: *The Role of the Individual in History** (Moscow, Foreign Languages Publishing House, 1944, 62 pp.). This is Plekhanov's orthodox defense of the monistic interpretation of history in which history is determined not by personalities but by the material economic modes of production.

George Plekhanov: *Fundamental Problems of Marxism** (New York, International Publishers, 1969, 190 pp.). In articulating the material causes of historical change, he emphasizes the geographical aspect as determing the development of economic forces and through them of all other social relations.

George Plekhanov: *In Defense of Materialism* (New York, International Publishers, 1967). In defending the materialist world view, he attacks the idealism of Berdyaev and Bulgakov, who were known as "God Seekers," and of Lunacharski and Gorki, who were known as "God Builders."

In being introduced to the Orthodox Marxists, the student should also become familiar with the name of Rosa Luxemburg (1870-1919), an articulate defender of orthodox Marxism who was militant against any revision of that thought, but whose independent mind did not hesitate to criticize orthodox Marxism. She became a vehement critic of Bolshevism and of Lenin in particular. Her most important thoughts are expressed in:

Rosa Luxemburg: *The Russian Revolution and Leninism or Marxism*, (Ann Arbor, Univ. of Michigan Press, 1962, 109 pp.). In defense of revolution by the democratic process, she attacks the Russian revolution as a violation of Marxist principles by substituting the dictatorship of the Party for the dictatorship of the proletariat.

Other intellectuals were convinced that the philosophy of Marx and Engels must be viewed as a dynamic doctrine to be revised and adjusted to the changing conditions of an evolving world. The term Revisionist applied first to Eduard Bernstein (1850-1932), the classic spokesman for the trend, but it later became a title of opprobrium for anyone who pretended to interpret any doctrine of Marx or Engels in a manner different from that of the Marxists. Finally in Russia it has been applied to anyone guilty of the heresy of disagreeing with Lenin and, after him, the Party. For a study of revisionism in its broadest sense see:

Leopold Labedz (ed.): *Revisionism, Essays on the History of Marxist Ideas** (New York, Praeger, 1962, 404 pp.). A collection of studies by experts, this volume covers the whole history of revisionism from Bernstein to the New Left.

For the classical statement of the theories of revisionism the following book by Bernstein should be read:

Eduard Bernstein: *Evolutionary Socialism** (New York, Schocken Books, 1961, 224 pp.). Rejecting economic determinism, Bernstein denies the inevitability of the laws of economic development of history. He finds the motivating factor of the socialist revolution to be more a Kantian ethical principle than a principle of the so-called dialectic in practice.

5

SOVIET MARXISM-LENINISM

Marxism-Leninism rests on the ideological base of the writings of Marx and Engels as interpreted and revised by V. I. Lenin and Soviet philosophers. The Marxist-Leninist tradition continues to be developed today by a large number of scholars and philosophers, especially in the Soviet Union. Most of the contemporary work in Marxism-Leninism appears in Russian, and since little is translated, the student who wishes to do advanced work in contemporary Marxism-Leninism (an M.A. thesis, for example) must, of necessity, know the language.

Soviet Marxism-Leninism has gone through four basic stages. From 1917-1921, the faculties of philosophy were purged of "bourgeois" influences. Lenin dominated this period of change from classical Russian philosophy to Marxist-Leninist philosophy. During the second period, 1922-1931, this change was more firmly established with the founding of the Institute of Red Professors and the founding of a theoretical journal, *Under the Banner of Marxism*. A running fight also developed between those who interpreted Marxism-Leninism mechanistically and those who took a more Hegelian view. The discussion was ended by Stalin's decree of 1931. A middle-of-the-road interpretation was established as official. The years 1931-1947 saw little philosophical discussion of any value. Stalin's *On Dialectical and Historical Materialism* became the official Soviet text. Soviet philosophers limited themselves to quoting and commenting on Marx, Engels, Lenin, and Stalin. In 1947, A. A. Ždanov, representing Stalin, told the philosophers to discuss philosophical questions more freely and to be more belligerent toward non-Marxist-Leninist philosophers.

Since then, Soviet Marxism-Leninism has developed markedly. It discusses many problems of real philosophical value and interest.

The following four works provide the beginner with a clear presentation of the place of Marxism-Leninism in the total spectrum of Marxism and of the development of Soviet philosophical thought:

R. N. C. Hunt: *The Theory and Practice of Communism** (Baltimore, Penguin, 1963, 315 pp.). This is an excellent critical introduction which covers philosophical, economic, historical, and political aspects of the development of Marxism-Leninism from the Marxian basis up to 1956. Shapiro's preface to the Penguin edition mentions the developments since the 1956 de-Stalinization in Russia. Thus the book as a whole presents a good overview for the beginning student.

H. B. Acton: *The Illusion of the Epoch, Marxism-Leninism As a Philosophical Creed* (London, Cohen & West, 1962, 278 pp.). This work is an excellent presentation and critique of the philosophical core of Marxism-Leninism as found in the works of Marx, Engels, Lenin, and Stalin. It deals with problems of ontology and theory of knowledge and some of the basic premises of Marxist ethics and historical materialism. The sophistication of the analysis makes the book appropriate only for a beginner who already is fairly well grounded in either philosophy or political theory.

After reading one of the above two works, which are based only upon the classics of Marxism-Leninism, the student should turn to one of the following, which are introductions to the Soviet development of the Marxist-Leninist tradition:

Joseph M. Bochenski: *Soviet Russian Dialectical Materialism* (Dordrecht, Reidel, 1963, 174 pp.). This is a brief and clear introduction to Soviet philosophy, with an emphasis on dialectical materialism. Of special value are the sections on the philosophical and cultural background, the sketch of the development of philosophy in the Soviet Union up to 1956, and some interesting appendices on the more concrete aspects of Soviet practice of philosophy.

Gustav Wetter: *Soviet Ideology Today, Dialectical and Historical Materialism* (London, Heinemann, 1966, 334 pp.). The author presents the philosophical doctrines of Soviet ideology, mainly as they are found in two officially sanctioned textbooks published in the late 1950s. The three parts of the book discuss dialectical materialism, historical materialism, and the political economy of capitalism. There is a criticism following each chapter. This book is the best source for acquiring a knowledge of the core of common philosophical beliefs held today in the Soviet Union.

There is one study which stands out from all the rest by its comprehensive treatment of the development and contemporary situation in Soviet philosophy. It is a very detailed work, and should be read by the beginner only after he has acquired a basic knowledge from one of the abovementioned books, but it is the standard work in the field and can always be consulted with profit:

Gustav Wetter: *Dialectical Materialism, A Historical and Systematic Survey of Philosophy in the Soviet Union* (New York, Praeger, 1963, 609 pp.). Part one of this book is a historical treatment beginning with Hegel, and proceeding to Marx, Engels, Lenin, 19th century Russian thought, and the development of 20th century Soviet philosophy. Part two is a systematic account of the Soviet discussions in the basic subdivisions of dialectical materialism, such as the theory of matter, the dialectic, and theory of knowledge.

V. I. Lenin

V. I. Lenin (1870-1924), the founder of Soviet Marxism-Leninism, was a lawyer by profession and a member of the revolutionary wing of the Russian intelligentsia. He was forced into exile in Western Europe where he continued to devote his life to adapting Marxism to Russian conditions and bringing about a Bolshevik revolution in Russia. He returned from exile after the Czar was overthrown and led a coup against the socialist revolution.

Some of Lenin's contributions to the Marxist tradition are: (a) his theory of an elite vanguard party, (b) his theory of the internationalization of the revolutionary struggle and hence his notion that the revolution could occur first in an economically backward country, (c) his "reflection" theory of knowledge. As one works through the Marxian, the Marxist, and the Marxist-Leninist writings he must consider whether Marx's own thought was developed or distorted in the hands of Lenin. The acceptance or rejection of Lenin is a basic difference dividing large numbers of people who maintain that they are followers of Marx.

The student can discover quite adequately both the place of Lenin in the development of Western thought and a substantial part of his thought by starting with an encyclopedia article and then the following paperback:

Robert Payne: *The Life and Death of Lenin** (New York, Avon Books, 1967, 708 pp.). This is an excellent and thorough biography of Lenin which gives an analysis of many of his writings and locates them in their historical and political context. The first chapter discusses Lenin's place in Russian intellectual history.

Since many of the differences between the thought of Marx and Lenin are due to Lenin's Russian background, the student should read carefully those sections of the books by Bochenski (*Soviet Russian Dialectical Materialism*) and Wetter (*Dialectical Materialism*) which treat of this. For a more detailed orientation, the following works can be consulted:

Nicholas Berdyaev: *The Origin of Russian Communism** (Ann Arbor, Univ. of Michigan Press, 1962, 191 pp.). This work by a famous Russian thinker is a classic statement of the peculiarly Russian features in Soviet Marxism-Leninism. He maintains that the lack of a critical tradition accounts for a dogmatism in Russian intellectual history in general and in the Soviet brand of Marxism in particular.

V. V. Zenkovsky: *A History of Russian Philosophy** (London, Routledge & Kegan Paul Ltd., 1953, 947 pp. in 2 vols.) This history is an excellent general survey of Russian philosophy. The introductory chapters are of particular help in seeing the basic difference between Russian and Western philosophy. It is recommended for those whose interest has been aroused by the Berdyaev book.

Because Lenin's principal importance in the Marxist tradition is in the area of political thought and revolutionary tactics and because most of the contemporary interest in Lenin is due to his political successes and political writings, the student could start with some of the works in the following set:

> *Lenin's Selected Works in Three Volumes* (New York, International Publishers, 1967, 2564 pp.).

The following works in this set are of great importance:

> *The Three Sources and Three Component Parts of Marxism* presents Lenin's threefold division of Marxism into philosophy, political economy, and scientific socialism. This division is still operative in Marxism-Leninism. Despite the division, all three parts are treated philosophically.

> *What Is to Be Done?* gives a detailed discussion of the necessity of a conspiratorial party of professional revolutionaries to seize power.

> *Imperialism, The Highest Stage of Capitalism* moves the revolutionary struggle from the national arena as Marx described it in *Capital* to the international arena.

> *The Proletarian Revolution and the Renegade Kautsky* is of particular interest to those who have read Karl Kautsky's *The Dictatorship of the Proletariat*. Lenin's work is a counterattack on Kautsky. Kautsky's work initiated a polemical series of five books which are attacks on and defenses of the Bolshevik Revolution. Lenin wrote the first defense and Trotsky wrote the second. The series is available in Ann Arbor Books, University of Michigan Press paperbacks.

There are only two works in Lenin's writings that are detailed investigations and studies in philosophy, and they are not contained in the above three-volume set:

V. I. Lenin: *Materialism and Empirio-Criticism** (New York, International Publishers, 1970, 397 pp.). This work, hailed by the Soviets as the "supreme philosophical achievement of Marxism" is Lenin's most significant contribution in philosophy. In a polemic directed against the Neo-Kantian influence in Russian Marxism and certain trends in the interpretation of modern physics, Lenin takes up two themes: the nature of knowledge and the concept of matter. As the Marxist solutions, Lenin proposes his "reflection" or copy theory of knowledge, and a distinction between the scientific and the philosophical concepts of matter. This important work should be studied by anyone who wishes to investigate the more properly philosophical aspects of Marxism.

V. I. Lenin: *Philosophical Notebooks* (vol. 38 of the *Collected Works*, Moscow, Foreign Languages Publishing House, 1961, 638 pp.). A collection of Lenin's notes not written for publication, these consist of comments on books read by Lenin from 1914-1916. They are important mainly for the emphasis which Lenin places on the Hegelian dialectic; that the dialectic will always remain a significant element of Soviet philosophy was assured here. Because of this work's unsystematic nature, it would be of interest only to the advanced student of Lenin.

Joseph Stalin

Joseph Stalin's (1879-1953) contribution to Marxist-Leninist philosophy is neither profound nor extensive, and since 1956 his works have been rather difficult to obtain. After reading the *Encyclopedia Britannica* article, the student could go to the following biography:

Robert Payne: *The Rise and Fall of Stalin** (New York, Avon Books, 1965, 864 pp.). The student of philosophy will not find anything of

original value in the writings of Stalin, but this paperback is a good
political biography and includes remarks on Stalin's writings.

There are only two works by Stalin that are concerned with
philosophy:

Joseph Stalin: *Dialectical and Historical Materialism** (New York,
International Publishers, 1940, 48 pp.). This work originally
appeared as a chapter in the *Short Course in the History of
the Communist Party (Bolshevik)*. Its formulation of dialectical
and historical materialism was slavishly followed by Soviet philosophers during the latter half of the Stalinist reign. An important innovation was the strong emphasis on the active role of
the superstructure in furthering social development and the introduction of the notion of a "revolution from above," i.e., one led by
the Party.

Joseph Stalin: *Marxism and Linguistics* (New York, International
Publishers, 1951). This is an important work for the history of the
Stalinist era of Soviet philosophy. In removing linguistics from the
ideological superstructure, Stalin introduced the principle that not
every academic discipline must be ideological.

Soviet Philosophy

The contemporary era of Soviet Philosophy begins, as noted above,
with Ždanov's speech in 1947. It is much more creative, and thus more
interesting for the philosopher, than the preceeding periods. Having mas-
tered one or more of the basic introductory works noted above, the
student should turn to the following works. These are official translations
of books which present the current approved line on the basic doctrines of
Soviet Marxism-Leninism:

Fundamentals of Marxism-Leninism (Moscow, Foreign Languages
Publishing House, 1963, 735 pp.). *Fundamentals* is a translation of

the basic textbook of Marxism-Leninism used in the Soviet Union. It is a clear and comprehensive explanation of basic doctrines in five parts: dialectical materialism, historical materialism, the political economy of capitalism, the theory and tactics of the international Communist movement, and scientific communism. This book is the best place for a beginner to start studying primary Soviet sources.

If the *Fundamentals of Marxism-Leninism* is not available, the student can get a good idea of its contents from the following work:

Helmut Fleischer: *Short Handbook of Communist Ideology* (Dordrecht, Reidel, 1965, 98 pp.). This is an excellent brief synopsis of the *Fundamentals*; its main doctrines are summarized in its own terms, without comment. A useful subject index is appended.

Another translation of a Soviet work which is most helpful to the beginner is:

M. Rosenthal and P. Yudin (eds.): *A Dictionary of Philosophy* (Moscow, Progress Publishers, 1967, 494 pp.). The dictionary format makes this work very handy for a student looking for a specific point of Marxist-Leninist doctrine. Thus it is a useful supplement to the *Fundamentals*. One could, if necessary, use the *Dictionary* as a replacement for the *Fundamentals* by looking up a few entries and pursuing cross references. All of the entries are concise and clearly written, making the book valuable for the beginner.

In addition to the comprehensive *Fundamentals*, there are a large number of Soviet texts translated into English which deal with specific facets of Marxism-Leninism. All of these translations follow the official line, and although they go into somewhat more detail on specific aspects of Marxism-Leninism than the *Fundamentals*, they remain on a basic-to-intermediate level of discussion. Most are in paperback editions. The following are among the best ones currently available:

V. Afanasyev: *Marxist Philosophy, A Popular Outline* (Moscow,

Progress Publishers, 1968, 365 pp.). This work is a concise statement of all of the basic doctrines of dialectical and historical materialism. Although somewhat superficial, it is clear and straightforward. An added feature, unusual in Soviet books, is a name and subject index. This seems to be the only Soviet work in English covering the same area as the untranslated *Fundamentals of Marxist Philosophy*, the basic philosophical textbook in the Soviet Union.

For the student who is interested primarily in the metaphysical and epistemological conceptions of Soviet philosophy (dialectical materialism), the following original work can be recommended:

G. Kursanov (ed.): *Fundamentals of Dialectical Materialism* (Moscow, Progress Publishers, 1967, 323 pp.). A collective work, written by six leading Soviet philosophers, this is relatively detailed and philosophically sophisticated. It deals only with the problems of dialectical materialism: matter, dialectics, the categories, knowledge, science. For example, over sixty pages are devoted to the theory of knowledge.

The main lines of Marxism-Leninism's social philosophy, known as historical materialism, are presented competently in the following two studies:

An Outline of Social Development* (Moscow, Progress Publishers, 365 pp. in 2 vols.) Vol. I deals with pre-capitalist formations; Vol. II with capitalist societies and the transition to Communist society. The Marxist-Leninist theory of the nature and process of social progress is presented in detail. The authors take time to define certain basic concepts, such as force and relations of production.

G. Glezerman: *The Laws of Social Development** (Moscow, Foreign Languages Publishing House, 1960, 279 pp.). The author, one of the deans of Soviet philosophy, here grapples with the central problem of historical materialism: the nature of historical laws of society. He discusses, among other things, the cognition of social laws, their relation to conscious activity, the interaction of general and specific laws, and the law-bound character of the transition to socialism.

The branch of Soviet ideology called scientific socialism deals with the last two stages of history—socialism and Communism proper—and the problems connected with their explanation. Three of these problems receive much attention in contemporary Soviet philosophy: the transition from socialism to Communism, the role technology has to play in this development, and the character of the future Communist society. The following works will give the student a good overview of the Soviet treatment of these matters:

L. Minayev: *Origin and Principles of Scientific Socialism** (Moscow, Progress Publishers, 1967, 142 pp.). This is a brief treatment of the transition to Communism, the laws of the development of Communist society, and the nature of that society.

V. Afanasyev: *Scientific Communism, A Popular Outline* (Moscow, Progress Publishers, 1967, 344 pp.). Afansyev is one of the most prolific Soviet writers on scientific communism. This work covers the same material as Minayev's book, but in much greater detail.

G. Volkov: *Era of Man or Robot?** (Moscow, Progress Publishers, 1967, 181 pp.). This work is an analysis of technology, its development, and its impact on society. It offers a clear statement of how progressing technology influences man's life and leads to the Communist society.

Man, Science, and Society (Moscow, Progress Publishers, 1965, 316 pp.). After a basic introduction to Marxism-Leninism, the authors turn to the notion of the new man in the Communist society, including elements of both social being and social consciousness. It treats the wonders of the Communist society in a rather pedestrian fashion, but shows a working example of the relationships Soviet philosophers are obliged to find between social being and social consciousness.

Unfortunately, most of the Soviet works translated into English are popular presentations or ideological polemics; very few specialized studies in philosophy have been translated. There are only a few exceptions:

P. V. Tavanec (ed.): *Problems of the Logic of Scientific Knowledge* (Dordrecht, Reidel, 1970, 429 pp.). The editor selects articles by contemporary Soviet philosophers dealing with problems, especially epistemological, in the philosophy of science.

A. A. Zinov'ev: *Foundations of the Logical Theory of Scientific Knowledge* (Dordrecht, Reidel, 1970, 310 pp.). Zinov'ev is one of the leading Soviet logicians. He presents here a highly technical argument.

Karl Marx and Modern Philosophy* (Moscow, Progress Publishers, 1968, 240 pp.). This collection of articles is particularly interesting since it shows the changing Soviet attitude to the works of the young Marx. It contains articles on Marx by B. M. Kedrov, T. I. Ojzerman, H. G. Batishchev, and other important Soviet philosophers. Batishchev contributes a highly interesting article on alienation.

There is one quarterly (cited previously in "Introduction") devoted almost exclusively to translations of Soviet articles in philosophy; this may serve the student as a source for original texts on special problems:

Soviet Studies in Philosophy (New York, International Arts and Sciences Press).

The studies of Soviet philosophy produced in the West are not very numerous. The student should always be careful in turning to a book or article claiming to discuss "Soviet" philosophy, for many of these are written by authors who have no knowledge of Russian and must therefore depend on the scanty and unrepresentative translations available. Among the few competent studies which exist, the above-mentioned works by J. M. Bochenski (*Soviet Russian Dialectical Materialism*, Dordrecht, Reidel, 1963) and G. A. Wetter (*Dialectical Materialism*, New York, Praeger,

1963) are standard works. The latter is a very detailed presentation of the Soviet discussions in the area of dialectical materialism. More specialized studies by competent scholars include the following:

Thomas J. Blakeley: *Soviet Scholasticism* (Dordrecht, Reidel, 1961, 176 pp.). This is a philosophical investigation of the "theological" nature of Soviet philosophy. It charges that the assent Communists give to Marxist-Leninist theory is based on an act of faith rather than on empirical proof.

Thomas J. Blakeley: *Soviet Theory of Knowledge* (Dordrecht, Reidel, 1964, 203 pp.). The author presents a description of the main categories and principles used by Soviet philosophers in dealing with the nature of knowledge, methods and methodology, and the history of epistemology.

Guy Planty-Bonjour: *The Categories of Dialectical Materialism, Contemporary Soviet Ontology* (Dordrecht, Reidel, 1967, 182 pp.). The author describes and analyzes the basic categories and principles of the emerging Soviet ontology. After a general discussion of the nature and relation of the categories, he analyzes the concept of matter, the laws of the dialectic, causality, and finality.

E. Laszlo (ed.): *Philosophy in the Soviet Union. A Survey of the Mid-Sixties* (Dordrecht, Reidel, 1967, 208 pp.). This work brings together essays on some problems now being discussed by Soviet philosophers: truth, values, knowledge, logic, psychology, law, social structure, etc. It represents the latest results of the research of leading scholars in the field.

T. R. Payne: *S. L. Rubinstejn and the Philosophical Foundations of Soviet Psychology* (Dordrecht, Reidel, 1968, 184 pp.). This valuable work traces the history of Soviet psychology from its 19th century sources up to about 1964, but the larger part of the book is devoted to an analysis of the philosophical psychology of S. L. Rubenstejn. Three main problems receive concentrated discussion: the nature of the psychic, the relation of the psychic to the external world, and the relation of psychic activity to the brain.

Richard T. DeGeorge: *Soviet Ethics and Morality** (Ann Arbor, Univ. of Michigan Press, 1969, 173 pp.). DeGeorge presents a penetrating analysis and critique of the leading principles of Soviet ethics, bringing to bear on this the analytic tools of contemporary ethical theory.

Peter Kirschenmann:*Information and Reflection, On Some Problems of Cybernetics and How Contemporary Dialectical Materialism Copes with Them.* (Dordrecht, Reidel, 1970, 225 pp.). The first half of the book is a clear and expert introduction to cybernetics and the philosophical problems involved in this new science. The rest of the book deals with how contemporary Soviet philosophers are trying to meet the challenge of these problems.

George L. Kline: *Religious and Anti-Religious Thought in Russia* (Chicago, Univ. of Chicago Press, 1968, 179 pp.). The author gives a competent and eminently readable account of the religious elements in the thought of Bakunin, Tolstoy, Leontyev, Rozanov, Shestov, Berdyaev, and others with a chapter on the "God Builders" (Lunacharski and Gorki) and another on Plekhanov and Lenin.

George Fischer (ed.): *Science and Ideology in Soviet Society* (New York, Atherton, 1967, 176 pp.). Four eminent Sovietologists examine recent Soviet sociology, philosophy, cybernetics, and economics and come to the conclusion that Communist ideology has been able to adapt to threats from these disciplines.

Several journals specializing in Soviet and East European studies contain valuable articles on contemporary developments. Their book review sections should also be consulted for references to recent Soviet works:

Survey, A Journal of Soviet and East-European Studies (London, Summit House, 1950 ff.). This quarterly contains occasional articles and reviews of interest to philosophers.

Problems of Communism (Washington, D. C., United States Information Agency, 1952 ff.). This is a bi-monthly journal which emphasizes the practice of Communism, with occasional articles of interest to philosophers. There is an author and title index in each issue and an annual cumulative index.

Slavic Review, American Quarterly of Soviet and East European Studies (Univ. of Illinois, American Association for the Advancement of Slavic Studies, 1941 ff.). This journal covers the history, literature, politics, economics, and philosophy in Soviet and East European countries. It contains occasional articles and reviews of interest to philosophers. It is indexed yearly and quarterly by author and title. There is a valuable cumulative index to 1941-1964, which includes an index by subject matter.

Studies in Soviet Thought (Dordrecht, Reidel, 1960 ff.). This quarterly is dedicated to Soviet and East European philosophy. Subject and name indices appear biennially. An important feature of this journal is its running bibliography of Soviet philosophy, which lists all current Soviet works in philosophy. Combined with the seven volumes of the *Bibliographie der Sowjetischen Philosophie* (Dordrecht, Reidel, 1959-1968), it provides complete bibliography of Soviet philosophical production from 1947 to the present.

Soviet books and periodicals can be purchased from Four Continents Bookstore, 156 Fifth Avenue, New York, New York 10010; Victor Kamlein Bookstore, 1410 Columbia Road, Washington, D. C.; Modern Bookstore, 3230 North Broadway, Chicago, Illinois 60657; or Imported Publications, 1730 Arcade Place, Chicago, Illinois 60612.

6
NEO-MARXISM

Marx's thought has been developed along several major paths. Engels and Lenin developed what has come to be called Marxism-Leninism. The classical revisions of Eduard Berstein, Karl Kautsky, and others were a reaction to this development, particularly from a Neo-Kantian perspective. More recently, especially since the publication of Marx's *The Economic and Philosophical Manuscripts* and *The German Ideology*, a third major trend has developed which is called Neo-Marxism. We have already considered the Marxist-Leninists and classical revisionists in the two previous chapters; now we shall turn to the Neo-Marxists.

The Neo-Marxists generally tend to reject dialectical materialism and its founders, Engels and Lenin. They concentrate on the humanism in the young Marx rather than on his later economic thought. The notion of alienation takes precedence over the notion of exploitation.

The division between the different paths of development is not always clear cut. For example, creative Marxist thinkers such as Georg Lukacs, Adam Schaff, and Louis Althusser would best be located on the Marxist-Leninist side, but just at the border with Neo-Marxism. Those in Eastern Europe who are more clearly Neo-Marxist would include Leszek Kolakowski, Ernst Bloch, Karel Kosik, Ivan Svitak, and Gajo Petrovic, The Neo-Marxists of Western Europe and America would include Erich Fromm, Lucien Goldmann, Raya Dunayevskaya, Herbert Marcuse (see chapter 8, "The New Left"), and others.

Neo-Marxism is generally anthropocentric (man-centered), while earlier Marxism and present Soviet Marxism-Leninism leans toward a cosmocentric view. Curiously enough, the anthropocentric view was strongly hinted at by two men who were not even familiar with the major writings of the Young Marx. They are the Italian, Antonio Labriola (1843-1904), and the Hungarian, Georg Lukacs (1885-). Although a student may want to begin his study with a more contemporary Neo-Marxist, the writings of Labriola and Lukacs are classics in the field and deserve careful attention:

Antonio Labriola: *Essays on the Materialistic Conception of History* (New York, Monthly Review Press, 1966, 246 pp.).

Georg Lukacs: *History and Class Consciousness* (Cambridge, MIT Press, 1971). This is a remarkable piece of Marxian scholarship because Lukacs anticipates many of the thoughts contained in Marx's *Economic and Philosophical Manuscripts*, although he did not know this work at the time.

In order for the student to orient himself in the general area of Neo-Marxism, he might first profitably consult:

L. Labedz (ed.): *Revisionism, Essays on the History of Marxist Ideals* (New York, Praeger, 1962, 386 pp.). Labedz has followed the Soviet convention in the title of his book; nevertheless, he presents a useful introduction to the "revisionists," from Bernstein to the present. The essays are arranged in four parts: Revolution Revisited; Personality, Truth and History; The New Revisionism; and The New Left. Part II is the most helpful as an introduction to some of the main themes of Neo-Marxism.

For an orientation to recent developments in Eastern Europe, the student will find helpful information in the following article:

Iring Fetscher: "New Tendencies in Marxist Philosophy" (in *East Europe*, vol. 16, No. 5, New York, May, 1967, pp. 9-14).

Also consult the *Encyclopedia of Philosophy* for a discussion of the philosophical developments in Poland, Czechoslovakia, and Yugoslavia. The articles are under the names of each country and are written by experts.

European Theorists

Once the student has oriented himself he should turn to the key Neo-Marxist thinkers. The following are sample selections, primarily from Eastern Europe:

> Leszek Kolakowski: *Toward a Marxist Humanism, Essays on the Left Today** (New York, Grove Press, 1968, 220 pp.). This is an excellent place to begin one's study of Neo-Marxism. Kolakowski, likening himself to a jester at the court of Marxian philosophy, says,
> > "We opt for a vision of the world that offers us the burden of reconciling in our social behavior those opposites that are the most difficult to combine: goodness without universal toleration, courage without fanaticism, intelligence without discouragement, and hope without blindness."
>
> Such is the direction taken by Kolakowski in this collection of essays which treats such topics as truth, hope, responsibility, and social progress.

Another excellent study of his is the following:

> Leszek Kolakowski: *The Alienation of Reason: A History of Positivist Thought** (New York, Doubleday, 1968).

Adam Schaff is another leading Polish philosopher, who like Kolakowski has fallen into disfavor with the Polish Communist Party. Schaff has contributed two important works:

> Adam Schaff: *A Philosophy of Man* (New York, Monthly Review Press, 1963, 139 pp.). Schaff recognizes the absence in Marxism of an adequate statement on the nature of the individual, yet he does not want to allow existentialism to fill the void. The danger seemed to be real, since in 1957 Jean-Paul Sartre had published in a Polish magazine an article entitled "Marxism and Existentialism" which produced deep philosophical reverberations. In his work, Schaff sketches a Marxian philosophy of man in relation to such topics as freedom, life, responsibility, and happiness.

Adam Schaff: *Marxism and the Human Individual* (intro. by E. Fromm, New York, McGraw-Hill, 1970, 268 pp.). In this work Schaff develops further the themes from his earlier book. He points out the centrality of the individual and admits that this ideal has not been reached under socialism; socialism itself is guilty of perpetrating certain types of human alienation. This work is an excellent example of a Marxist who realizes that the categories of exploitation must be situated in the broader context of the nature of human alienation.

A work which will help orient the student to the Polish philosophical scene, although it does not include the most recent developments, is the following:

Z. A. Jordan: *Philosophy and Ideology, The Development of Philosophy and Marxism-Leninism in Poland Since the Second World War* (Dordrecht, Reidel, 1963, 600 pp.). This is an expert and thoroughly documented account of the meeting between Marxism-Leninism and the indigenous, mainly analytical Polish tradition and of the adjustments made by both sides.

In Germany, Jürgen Habermas is currently the philosopher whose work has most interested Neo-Marxist theorists:

Jürgen Habermas: *Knowledge and Human Interest* (Boston, Beacon, 1971). In this work, Habermas expands Marcuse's idea of eros into interpersonal subjectivity based upon language communication. He brings a new involvement of Freud, hermeneutics, and linguistics into the Marcusian scene.

Except for one or two exceptions, East Germany is a wasteland as far as Neo-Marxism is concerned. One of the exceptions, Ernst Bloch, found he could not do the creative work he wished while in East Germany, so he left and now is professor of philosophy at the University of Tübingen in West Germany. His voluminous work, *The Principle of Hope*, currently being translated into English, is a creative piece of Marxist reflection. Two of Bloch's works are available in English:

Ernst Bloch: *A Philosophy of the Future* (New York, Herder and Herder, 1970, 149 pp.). This is a collection of lectures given at Tübingen. Throughout the work, Bloch develops one of his central themes, the hope of a secular utopia. Bloch believes that hope offers the source of power to transcend the given situation in such a way to make his utopia possible.

Ernst Bloch: *Man on His Own, Essays in the Philosophy of Religion* (New York, Herder and Herder, 1970, 240 pp.).

We have less access to contemporary thought in Hungary. For an overview of the recent philosophical developments in Hungary, consult:

Ervin Laszlo: *The Communist Ideology in Hungary, Handbook for Basic Research* (Dordrecht, Reidel, 1966, 351 pp.). Laszlo offers a historical introduction to the study of Marxism-Leninism in Hungary, followed by a systematic survey of what Hungarian philosophers are now doing. It inclues a Who's Who and a copious bibliography.

Recent events in Czechoslovakia have stirred the world. In order to gain an insight into the kind of philosophical reflection which was alive in Czechoslovakia before August 1968, turn to the following:

Ivan Svitak: *Man and His World, A Marxian View** (New York, Delta Books, 1968, 179 pp.). This is an excellent example of the creative thinking which helped inspire Czechoslovakian Marxism with a "human face." It is a strong defense of Marxist humanism and consists of a collection of articles dealing with the art of philosophy, alienation, man and poetry, and the meaning of Marxism.

Karel Kosik is recognized as one of the most creative Czechoslovakian Neo-Marxists. His *Dialectics of the Concrete* has yet to be translated into English. This is a significant work because of Kosik's desire to integrate Heidegger into Marxian thought. It is possible to get a feeling for the direction of Kosik's thought in an article:

Karel Kosik: "The Individual and History" (in *Marx and The Western World*, ed. by Lobkowicz, Notre Dame, Univ. of Notre Dame Press, 1967, pp. 177-190, 195-196).

Yugoslavia has produced a number of very able Neo-Marxist thinkers. Among them is Gajo Petrovic:

Gajo Petrovic: *Marx in the Mid-Twentieth Century** (New York, Doubleday, 1967, 230 pp.). This is probably the best example of contemporary Yugoslavian Neo-Marxist thought. Petrovic develops the thesis that the thought of the young Marx is not a juvenile sin of the genius who wrote *Capital*. He goes on to discuss Marx's concepts of man, freedom, praxis, alienation, and de-alienation.

Also worth consulting is Petrovic's article, "Alienation," in the *Encyclopedia of Philosophy* (1967, vol. I, pp. 76-81). Finally, in reference to Yugoslavia, the journal *Praxis* should be consulted regularly in order to follow the continued development of Yugoslavian Neo-Marxist thought.

There are two valuable anthologies which offer the student access to articles by both Eastern and Western European Neo-Marxists as well as other scholars of Marxism:

N. Lobkowicz (ed.): *Marx and the Western World** (Notre Dame, Univ. of Notre Dame Press, 1967, 444 pp.). This is a collection of papers presented at an International Symposium on Marxism held at the University of Notre Dame in April 1966.

E. Fromm (ed.): *Socialist Humanism** (New York, Doubleday, 1966, 461 pp.). Fromm classifies the articles in this collection under the themes: humanism, man, freedom, alienation, and practice. Before each article there is a biographical sketch of the author.

Marxism and Existentialism

Another aspect of contemporary Marxism is its encounter with existentialism. We have already mentioned Sartre's essay which was published in Poland in 1957, "Marxism and Existentialism." This appears in:

G. Novack (ed.): *Existentialism versus Marxism** (New York, Dell, 1966, 340 pp.). Novack's introduction and concluding essay will orient the student to Marxism's encounter with existentialism. Novack has also included articles by Simone de Beauvoir, Georg Lukacs, Roger Garaudy, Leszek Kolakowski, and others.

Sartre, in one of his later works, presented a new attempt to marry existentialism and Marxism:

Jean-Paul Sartre: *Search For a Method** (New York, Vintage Books, 1968, 181 pp.). This is only a portion of Sartre's lengthy work, which bears the title *Critique of Dialectical Reason*.

The following study can also be recommended:

Raymond Aron: *Marxism and the Existentialists** (New York, Clarion Books, 1970). Aron's five essays, written between 1946 and 1964, offer a rich look into the French intellectual's struggle to understand and appropriate Marx. Aron pays particular attention to Sartre's and Merleau-Ponty's encounters with Marxism.

Marxism and Freud

There are three works which consider Marx's relation to Freud. The student who is interested in both philosophy and psychology may want to consult them:

Reuben Osborn: *Marxism and Psycho-analysis** (New York, Dell, 1967, 160 pp.).

Herbert Marcuse: *Eros and Civilization** (Boston, Beacon, 1955, 256 pp.).

Erich Fromm: *Beyond the Chains of Illusion, My Encounter with Marx and Freud** (New York, Pocket Books, 1966, 182 pp.).

Marxist-Christian Dialogue

Given the rejuvenation of the Neo-Marxist interest in man and the Christian "discovery" of the secular world and the needs for social change, it is not surprising that a dialogue between persons in the two groups should have developed. This interest in dialogue has made very little headway into the areas where Marxism-Leninism dominates. It has been a phenomenon centered primarily in Eastern and Western Europe and more recently in the United States. One of the best introductions to the dialogue is to be found in:

T. Ogletree (ed.): *Openings for Marxist-Christian Dialogue* (Nashville, Abingdon Press, 1969, 174 pp.). Thomas Ogletree's introduction is an excellent place to begin. This volume also contains articles by Jurgen Moltmann, Charles West, Paul Lehmann, and Sidney Lens — all Christians.

An American Marxist has written an answer to this work:

Herbert Aptheker: *The Urgency of Marxist-Christian Dialogue, A Pragmatic Argument for Reconciliation** (New York, Harper and Row, 1970, 196 pp.). Aptheker re-evaluates Marx's attitude toward religion and distinguishes it from Lenin's.

One of the classic works in this area is by a French Marxist, Roger Garaudy, who was one of the pioneers in the dialogue:

Roger Garaudy: *From Anathema to Dialogue, A Marxist Challenge to the Christian Churches** (New York, Herder and Herder, 1966, 124 pp.). Garaudy responds to Pope John XXIII's openness for dialogue expressed in *Pacem in terris*. This is a strong plea for a new openness on the part of both Marxist and Christian. This plea has not gone unheard by Christian scholars.

A leading Catholic scholar has responded in the following work:

Frederick J. Adelmann: *From Dialogue to Epilogue, Marxism and Catholicism Tomorrow* (The Hague, Nijhoff, 1968, 89 pp.). Fr. Adelmann contends that the very points which prevented a dialogue earlier have to some extent been overcome by recent changes in Catholicism, matched by a new openness on the part of the Neo-Marxists.

For other articles by both Christians and Marxists, one can turn to:

P. Oestriecher (ed.): *The Christian Marxist Dialogue, An International Symposium** (New York, Macmillan, 1969, 301 pp.). Oestreicher presents a selection of articles which include Roger Garaudy, Helmut Gollwitzer, Johannes B. Metz, and a delightful piece by L. Kolakowski entitled "What Socialism is Not" (written in 1956).

In reconsidering the role of religion in our contemporary world and the Marxist attitude toward it, it is necessary to return to a careful consideration of Marx's and Engel's thoughts on religion. The Soviets have selected and published a number of excerpts from Marx's and Engel's writings, and this selection has been published in both countries:

Karl Marx and Friedrich Engels: *On Religion** (intro. by Reinhold Niebuhr, New York, Schocken, 1967, 382 pp.; Moscow, Foreign Languages Publishing House, 1957).

It is important to look closely at Marx's view of religion. An excellent treatment is:

Nicholas Lobkowicz: "Marx's Attitude Toward Religion" (in *Marx and The Western World*, ed. by N. Lobkowicz, Notre Dame, Univ. of Notre Dame Press, 1967, pp. 303-336).

There is a vast and developing literature in the field; therefore, if one is interested in studying the dialogue further he would best consult the excellent bibliography prepared in 1968:

> Douglas C. Stange: *The Nascent Marxist-Christian Dialogue: 1961-1967—A Bibliography* (New York, American Institute of Marxist Studies, 1968, 27 pp. mimeographed).

7

CHINESE MARXISM

Mao Tse-tung (1893-   ) is the founder of the Chinese Communist state and the present leader of the Chinese Communist Party. He was one of the early Chinese converts to Marxism-Leninism, and his political success ensured that his views would prevail in China. In fact, at present his interpretation of Marxism-Leninism is universally accepted there. In the West, his thought is referred to as "Maoism," but the Chinese themselves never use this phrase in official documents; it is always the "thought of Mao-Tse-tung." The philosophical thought of Mao has, unfortunately, not yet received much attention from Western philosophers. Most of the literature on Mao has been the work of political scientists, historians, and economists.

One of the best introductions to Mao's thought, and the book with which the student should begin, is:

Stuart R. Schram: *The Political Thought of Mao Tse-tung** (New York, Praeger, 1969, 479 pp.). This book consists of two parts. A long (135 page) introduction sketches the formation of Mao's thought and the transformation and development of China under Mao's leadership. Then selections from his writings are grouped together, with brief introductions, under nine headings, the second of which is "Mao Tse-tung as a Marxist Theoretician." By carefully reading the introduction and these selections, the student can orient himself in Mao's thought.

From the extensive writings of Mao himself, two articles stand out as explicit presentations of his philosophical thought: *On Practice* and *On Contradiction*. The student should take up these as his initial primary source material. They are available as separate booklets published by the Peking Foreign Languages Press or in:

Mao Tse-tung: *Four Essays on Philosophy** (Peking, Foreign Languages Press, 1966, 136 pp.). The article, *On Practice*, deals essentially with the theory of knowledge. In the essay, *Where Do Correct Ideas Come From*, Mao considers the question of obtaining true knowledge. The article, *On Contradiction*, is considered as Mao's version of the dialectic. The final essay in this collection, *On the Correct Handling of Contradiction Among the People*, is a practical application of his theory of contradiction to the solution of social problems, especially those which arose during the Hundred Flowers Campaign.

There are other anthologies of Mao's writings which may be of use to the student:

Mao Tse-tung: An Anthology of His Writings* (New York, Mentor, 1962, 300 pp.). This is a collection of Mao's important political and ideological articles, including *On Practice* and *On Contradiction*.

Winberg Chai (ed.): *Essential Works of Chinese Communism** (New York, Bantam, 1969, 464 pp.). Chai presents a wide selection of the important works of Chinese Communism from 1922 to 1968, with short introductory notes to each document. Unfortunately, the footnotes to these documents have been deleted.

Quotations from Chairman Mao Tse-tung* (Peking, Foreign Languages Press, 1967; New York, Bantam, 1967, 179 pp.). This anthology, often referred to as the "red book," contains groups of short, fragmentary statements extracted from Mao's speeches and writings. Ever since the outbreak of the Cultural Revolution, this book has been increasingly used for the propagation of Mao's thought and the furthering of social transformations in China.

For a more thorough study of Mao, the following source is indispensable:

Mao Tse-tung: *Selected Works of Mao Tse-tung** (Peking, Foreign Languages Press, vols. I-III, 1965, vol. IV, 1967; New York, International Publishers, vols. I-II, 1954; vol. III, 1955; vol. IV, 1956; vol. V, 1965). Contained here are Mao's important speeches, lectures, reports, articles, and essays on various topics and political events, from 1926 to 1949.

Mao's post-1949 writings have not yet been compiled in a single volume, even in Chinese. They lie scattered in the daily newspapers and periodicals of this period. Some of these writings can be found in English in the *Peking Review* or published in pamphlet form by the Peking Foreign Languages Press.

Among the discussions of Mao's thought by non-Maoist scholars, the following can be recommended:

Benjamin I. Schwartz: *Chinese Communism and the Rise of Mao** (Cambridge, Harvard Univ. Press, 1958, 258 pp.). This work gives a broad view of the historical development of Mao's thought and Chinese Communism during the early years of the Chinese Communist Revolution. The last chapter, "The Maoist Strategy," presents Maoism as a degenerate form of Marxism-Leninism.

Arthur Cohen: *The Communism of Mao Tse-tung** (Chicago, Univ. of Chicago Press, 1969, 210 pp.).

There are numerous articles to be found concerning Mao's social and political thought, military strategy, etc.; there are fewer which concern his philosophy. Of the following four articles, the first is a positive assessment and is highly recommended; the other three challenge the originality and quality of Mao's thought:

Vsevolod Honubnychy: "Mao Tse-tung's Materialistic Dialectics" (*The China Quarterly*, 1964, no. 19, pp. 3-37). The main thesis of the author is that "Mao's materialistic dialectics has a definite place of its own in the realm of Marxist-Leninist-Stalinist philosophy, because Mao's thought is a mixed product of Chinese culture and Marxism-Leninism."

R. I. Kosolapov: "The Thought of Mao Tse-tung: Renunciation of Marxism and Leninism" (*Soviet Studies in Philosophy*, vol. VIII, 1969, no. 1, pp. 3-25). The author is a Soviet philosopher. He articulates the current negative critique of Mao found in the Soviet Union, very much a part of the ideological Sino-Soviet split.

Karl A. Wittfogel: "Some Remarks on Mao's Handling of Concepts and Problems of Dialectics" (*Studies in Soviet Thought*, vol. III, 1963, no. 4, pp. 251-269). This article is followed by the first English translation of *On Dialectical Materialism*. Wittfogel challenges the originality of this work by tracing it to its Soviet sources.

Martin Glaberman: "Mao As a Dialectician" (*International Philosophical Quarterly*, vol. VIII, 1968, no. 1, pp. 94-112).

Two articles which are somewhat broader in scope, since they examine the state of Marxist-Leninist philosophy in China, are:

Jen Ch'o-hsuan: "The Introduction of Marxism-Leninism into China" (*Studies in Soviet Thought*, vol. X, 1970, pp. 136-166). This is a very short summary and introduction to the historical developments of Marxism-Leninism in China. The author was personally involved in many of the events.

K. T. Fann: "Philosophy in the Chinese Cultural Revolution" (*International Philosophical Quarterly*, vol. IX, 1969, no. 3, pp. 449-459). During and after the Cultural Revolution, materials became less accessible. However, as this article indicates, it seems that a new trend has emerged.

It is not possible to understand fully the thought of Mao without having a general idea of the philosophical and cultural tradition proper to

China. If the student wishes to pursue his enquiry at this point, the following general works will prove helpful:

H. G. Creel: *Chinese Thought, From Confucius to Mao Tse-tung** (New York, Mentor, 1960, 292 pp.). This rather simple and short presentation of the development of Chinese thought, written by a Western scholar, could well serve as an introduction.

Fung Yu-lan: *A History of Chinese Philosophy* (Princeton, Princeton Univ. Press, 1959-1960, 2 vols.). This is considered the most comprehensive and thorough history of Chinese philosophy to date. The author was basically a neo-Confucian in his early years; he later converted to Marxism in Mainland China. A shorter, condensed version of this work was published as *A Short History of Chinese Philosophy** (New York, The Free Press, 1966, 368 pp.).

Chan Wing-tsit (ed.): *A Source Book in Chinese Philosophy** (Princeton, Princeton Univ. Press, 1969, 856 pp.). This is one of the best anthologies covering the whole of Chinese philosophy. The last chapter deals specifically with Mao and contemporary Communist Chinese philosophers.

O. Briere: *Fifty Years of Chinese Philosophy, 1898-1948** (New York, Praeger, 1965, 159 pp.). This brief but comprehensive survey of contemporary Chinese philosophy is valuable insofar as it presents the immediate background of and includes Chinese Marxism.

Among the works which attempt to present a general picture of Chinese culture, rather than exclusively its philosophy, one of the following could serve to provide a general orientation:

Charles A. Moore (ed.): *The Chinese Mind: Essentials of Chinese Philosophy and Culture* (Honolulu, East-West Center Press, 1967, 402 pp.). This is a collection of papers presented at an East-West Philosophers Conference held at the University of Hawaii.

John K. Fairbank (ed.): *Chinese Thought and Institutions** (Chicago, Univ. of Chicago Press, 1967, 438 pp.). An anthology of papers delivered at symposia, this volume lays even more stress on the interaction between thought and institutions. The contributions take a social and historical approach rather than a purely philosophical one.

Finally, it might be noted that books and periodicals published in English and Chinese by the Peking Foreign Languages Press can be purchased from China Books and Periodicals, 2929 24th Street, San Francisco, California, 94110; or from Guozi Shudian, China Publications Center, P. O. Box 399, Peking, China.

8
THE NEW LEFT

The New Left is a sociopolitical movement rather than a philosophical school. Its members are generally less interested in the philosophical presuppositions and intellectual implications of their social programs than in the implementation of the programs themselves. They would not normally be recognized as philosophers. However, it is appropriate that they be mentioned in this book for two reasons: (a) There is, in fact, one New Left thinker who is a philosopher and whose works hold considerable interest — Herbert Marcuse. It is justifiable to call Marcuse "the" philosopher of the New Left, since his thought is at an incomparably higher theoretical level than that of the other members of the movement. (b) The publications of many other New Left authors, although they are not strictly philosophical in nature, nevertheless have been influenced strongly by different types of Marxist philosophy. Some of them accept totally the Marxist-Leninist or Maoist forms of Marxism.

There are two selections of articles that could serve as an introduction to the various trends in the New Left:

C. Oglesby (ed.): *New Left Reader** (New York, Grove Press, 1969, 312 pp.). Oglesby's introduction provides a clear and concise statement of the differences between the "Old Left" and the New Left. Selections are included from the writings of Castro, Cohn-Bendit, Dutschke, Fanon, Kolakowski, Marcuse, and Newton. Because of the introduction, this book seems like the best place to begin one's study of the New Left.

P. Long (ed.): *The New Left** (Boston, Porter Sargent, 1969, 475 pp.). This contains selections by many of the men in Oglesby's *Reader* and by other theoreticians such as Staughton Lynd. The book is divided into several sections by topic, and it includes one section specifically on New Left theory.

Herbert Marcuse

The works of Herbert Marcuse are the best the New Left has to offer. In spite of their difficulty, they have exerted great influence in academic and activist circles and have even achieved a certain vogue. These works, listed in the order of increasing difficulty, include:

Herbert L. Marcuse: *One Dimensional Man** (Boston, Beacon Press, 1964, 260 pp.). This work is a detailed critique of our modern technological society, sometimes called by the author the giant corporate-governmental-military complex. One-dimensionality means that persons in this society are falsely reduced to the state of happy consciousness by obliterating the natural contradictions in life. Positivism and the school of linguistic analysis come under heavy attack in a volume that does not present much of Marcuse's own positive program. This book is recommended first because it is the most widely read and the easiest for the beginning student to understand.

Herbert L. Marcuse: *Eros and Civilization** (New York, Random House, 1962). This particular edition has a new and important preface written by the author. There are three important influences in the thought of Marcuse: Hegel, Marx, and Freud. In this volume Marcuse discusses Freud and presents his own interpretation. In the opinion of some critics, this is Marcuse's most significant work.

Herbert L. Marcuse: *An Essay on Liberation** (Boston, Beacon Press, 1969, 91 pp.). A short and more recent statement of Marcuse's hopes for the future and his emphasis on participatory socialism. The style is clear and interesting as the author begins to be optimistic about the possibilities of his own ideas becoming actual. A necessary volume for the student of the New Left and of Marcuse in particular.

Herbert L. Marcuse: "Repressive Tolerance" (in *A Critique of Pure Tolerance* by Robert Wolff, Barrington Moore, Jr., and Herbert L. Marcuse, Boston, Beacon Press, 1965). All three essays in this book are both interesting and Marcusian. But in Marcuse's own essay we have something of his own positive program for the future, although his blueprint is always vague. The student will likely be surprised to find that Marcuse is willing to suppress what he considers the wrong kind of freedoms, namely those that allow the status quo free rein. This book is important, but requires of the reader careful analysis.

Herbert L. Marcuse: *Negations, Essays in Critical Theory** (Boston, Beacon, 1969, 290 pp.). These essays are heavy going for the student, but are the best place to learn Marcuse's later theory which is called Critical Theory. The essay on "The Concept of Essence" reveals Marcuse's deep and extensive philosophical background and indicates to what brief extent the author is in agreement with the Aristotelian notion of essence. For students who are acquainted with the writing of Norman O. Brown, there is an interesting exchange between the two men, presented in two short essays.

Since Marcuse is a contemporary, there are not yet many treatments of his thought, but two can be recommended:

Paul A. Robinson: *The Freudian Left: Wilhelm Reich, Geza Roheim, Herbert Marcuse** (New York, Harper and Row, 1969, pp. 147-244). The whole book offers valuable background material for an understanding of Marcuse. The pages given refer to the section especially devoted to Marcuse, who read it himself before the author published the volume. The book is indexed, and has copious footnote references to Marcuse's own writings. It reads rather easily and interestingly.

Robert W. Marks: *The Meaning of Marcuse** (New York, Ballantine Books, 1970, 147 pp.). The core of the book is a detailed analysis of some of Marcuse's more important writings, namely, *Reason and Revolution*, *Eros and Civilization*, *One Dimensional Man*, and *An Essay on Liberation*. In the introduction of this volume the student will find a brief biography of Marcuse together with a description of certain contemporary events that reveal the deep influence of Marcuse at home and abroad. There is an excellent bibliography at the end.

Programmatic Philosophy

The writings of the New Left are largely concerned with tactics and responses to concrete situations. Their practical programs thus differ from time to time from country to country. The following will be of interest to the student:

Daniel and Gabriel Cohn-Bendit: *Obsolete Communism, the Left-Wing Alternative** (New York, McGraw-Hill, 1968, 256 pp.). The constant counterpoint of Communist Party and New Left theories and tactics in this work helps to clarify in detail the differences between these two stances.

Regis Debray: *Revolution in the Revolution, Armed Struggle and Political Struggle in Latin America** (New York, Monthly Review Press, 1967, 126 pp.). In this work Debray shows the rationale of "urban guerilla" tactics by working out an analysis of the modern technological society.

The Black Panther Party is a variant on the American scene. In addition to a strong dose of classical Marxism-Leninism, the Panthers have been influenced by Marcuse and by Frantz Fanon:

Frantz Fanon: *The Wretched of the Earth** (New York, Grove Press, 1968, 316 pp.). Fanon's seminal work examines the psychological dynamics which would lead up to a "third-world" revolution.

For an introduction to Black Panther theory, consult:

P. S. Foner (ed.): *The Black Panthers Speak** (New York, Lippincott, 1970, 274 pp.). This is an up-to-date presentation of the various facets of the Black Panther program, with some emphasis on theory in the selections by Eldridge Cleaver and Huey Newton.

Eldridge Cleaver: *On the Ideology of the Black Panther Party. Part I.** (San Francisco, Black Panther Party, 1970, 13 pp.). This pamphlet by Cleaver emphasizes "the historical experience of Black people" and makes an explicit identification of Black Panther ideology with Marxism-Leninism.

No single theorist is outstanding in other American Left organizations, such as the Progressive Labor Party, the World Socialist Workers Party, the Weathermen, etc. Pamphlets put out by these groups are of occasional theoretical interest and are available at their local headquarters.

Anarchist Tradition

If one wishes to make a serious study of New Left thought, he must also acquaint himself with the anarchist tradition. Anarchism, especially as found in the positions of Michael Bakunin (1814-1876) and Peter Kropotkin (1842-1921), has exerted a strong influence on New Left thinkers. For an introduction, the two articles in the *Encyclopedia Britannica* on Bakunin and Kropotkin are highly recommended. They are written by Richard Hare, a recognized scholar. The two following selections give the student access to the original writings of these Russian anarchists:

Michael Bakunin: *The Political Philosophy of Bakunin** (ed. by G. P. Maximov, New York, Free Press). Maximov has selected Bakunin's most important works in political philosophy for this volume. It includes a good introduction by the editor.

Peter Kropotkin: *Kropotkin's Revolutionary Pamphlets** (ed. by R.

N. Baldwin, New York, Dover, 1970, 309 pp.). The paperback edition is simply a reprinting of a 1927 publication. There is no introduction.

INDEX

Authors and editors of books and articles are listed below; translators are not included. Page numbers represent the principal or annotated notation of the work; other mentions are not included.